CONCEPTIONS OF
Shakespeare

CONCEPTIONS OF
Shakespeare

ALFRED HARBAGE

HARVARD UNIVERSITY PRESS

CAMBRIDGE, MASSACHUSETTS · 1966

FOREWORD

*T*HIS BOOK brings together my offerings during the Shakespeare Quadricentenary: a series of five lectures together with several essays related to the lectures in theme. It is made up of material here printed for the first time and of reprinted material somewhat revised.

The title of the lectures was suggested by a surviving fragment of the liberal education once certified as mine. As a college undergraduate, I was required to earn six credits in the biological sciences, and having liberalized myself to the extent of three credits in Introductory Zoology, I elected a course in Introductory Psychology on the mistaken assumption that it would yield more human interest than the only alternative, Introductory Botany. We began by testing reflexes in the leg muscles of a frog, and ended by dissecting a quite-dead human brain, exploring in the interim the mechanism of the nervous system. Out of this scientific nettle I plucked one philosophic flower, labeled, as the reader may guess, the "afterimage." Staring at a *bright* circle indubitably caused a *dark* circle to appear on our retinas when we shut our eyes. Staring at a *red* square likewise left an "afterimage" which was not only different but different in a radical way, in fact a square of complementary *green*.

The official explanation of this odd phenomenon now eludes me, but I have not forgotten the depth of speculation stirred in my questing mind. In the literary society to which I belonged I made an issue of the afterimage, maintaining that it symbolized human perversity, perhaps even Original Sin. More moderate reflections succeeded in their usual way, and reckoned with the fact that afterimages do not wholly pervert images since size and shape remain constant even though color reverses. Conceivably, then, if the mind's eye of our kind once stares intently at greatness it will continue to see greatness whatever the new coloration. And even though it be part of our natures auto-defensively to resist all pressures, including the pressure of facts, still facts have a way of remaining available if we choose to reopen our eyes.

My theme is the Shakespearean image in after ages—the Shakespearean afterimage—as impinged on the retinas of biographers, critics, actors, theatrical directors, and thinkers, as discriminable although not necessarily mutually exclusive groups. It goes without saying that Shakespeare may not have been precisely the kind of man he is sometimes pictured as being, and that the original uses of his plays may have differed in certain particulars from the uses to which they are sometimes put. I am aware that my eyes are as apt to form deceptive afterimages as those of anyone else, and my discourse has not been composed in a mood of bitter reproof. The intention has been to provide the kind of retrospective review that might prove useful, and hence to include a certain amount of information as well as personal opinions.

The five lectures were delivered in April 1964, during a Shakespeare celebration sponsored collectively by Mount Mercy College, Chatham College, the University of Pittsburgh, the Carnegie Institute of Technology, and Duquesne University. I levied upon their material in less formal talks and group discussions later in the year at Ohio Wesleyan University, Oberlin College, Hiram College, and the Shakespeare Seminar presided over by Professor Barry Jackson in Stratford, Ontario. To my hosts, audiences, and fellow speakers on these various occasions I wish to offer my thanks. The lectures are here presented substantially as given in Pittsburgh except for "The Myth of Perfection." This is presented as revised for readers of *Shakespeare 400,* edited by Dr. James McManaway and published by Holt, Rinehart & Winston in

1964. The essay "Shakespeare as Culture Hero" represents the recasting of a Founder's Day Lecture delivered at the Huntington Library and published in a Shakespeare Memorial issue of the *Huntington Library Quarterly,* May 1964. "Shakespeare's Ideal Man" is an older piece newly documented as well as slightly revised; it originally appeared in the *Joseph Quincy Adams Memorial Studies* published by The Folger Shakespeare Library in 1948. I wish to thank the proprietors indicated above for permission to reprint.

The final piece has been included with some hesitation, and an explanation may be in order. It is a *jeu d'esprit* and tribute delivered as an after-dinner speech at the Shakespeare Memorial Banquet of the Shakespeare Association of America graciously conducted by Mrs. Mary Hyde. If that had been the end-all there, as I expected it to be, no explanation would be needed, but the piece was subsequently printed in the *Shakespeare Quarterly,* and I have since had several inquiries whether there was a chance of my finding more letters. Since I do not wish to share the peculiar fame of John Payne Collier, I must here state unequivocally that the letters are obvious forgeries by an apprentice hand. Further, since they seem to emanate from such a pious and homespun Shakespeare, some dubiety may arise about my own "after-image" of Shakespeare and qualifications to treat the subject objectively. So far as the piety is concerned, when we say that Shakespeare's writing is nonreligious, we really mean that it is nondenominational; and I have little doubt that in his ordinary discourse the usual phrases of Christian orthodoxy came as habitually from his lips as from those of practically all of his contemporaries. So far as the homespun quality is concerned, I am reminded of a remark about Spenser made by the late C. S. Lewis—that among the various Spensers suggested to us by his sometimes exotic works, we can discern a homespun, middle-class, "churchwardenly

Spenser." This strikes me as very true, and I think the same kind of statement may be even more true of Shakespeare. Still, these letters do not quite project my own afterimage of Shakespeare. I suspect that his dual role as Stratford burgher and London playwright may have spelled more wear and tear on the nerves than these letters would suggest.

A. H.

Cambridge, Massachusetts
January 1965

CONTENTS

THE SHAKESPEAREAN AFTERIMAGE

1 A LIFE OF ALLEGORY

*M*Y INITIAL topic is the Shakespearean biographers and the conceptions of Shakespeare the man formed with or without their aid. We know that Shakespeare was a particular man who lived in a particular time and place, and created a particular body of poems and plays. About the public facts—his birth, class, marriage, working career, and the like—we are reasonably well informed. About the private facts—the way he ate, dressed, bathed, and exercised his libido, indeed all those ultimate intimacies now ruthlessly exposed to the eyes of the world in biographies of modern authors—we are not informed at all. For this Charles Dickens[1] unabashedly cried "Thank God," to which I furtively murmur "Amen." Still, there remains a realm of inquiry lying somewhere between the impertinent and the impersonal which must be accepted as open. It is legitimate, or at least inevitable, that we should ask questions about his character and personality. What kind of man was he? What was he like?

The documented facts admit of no certain interpretation; they are, by and large, neutral. They prove, to be sure, that Shakespeare was neither criminal nor disablingly eccentric. He was able to function—to integrate in society, pursue a career, rear a family, and achieve a natural death. If we had the documents only, and neither his writings nor the remarks of his contemporaries, we would conclude that Shakespeare was not without blemish, was no saint, but that he was a respectable sort of citizen, probably above average in integrity and good sense as such things may be judged by the way in which people conduct their visible lives. When we turn from the strictly factual record to the fragmentary comment of his friends, we hear that Shakespeare was "civil," was "worthy," was "honest," was "gentle," that he was upright "in his dealings" and was "of an open and free nature." These are fine things to be, indeed the finest, and for this very reason we must bear in mind that we are listening to his friends. Perhaps the best validation of this kind of testimony is the fact that he did have *friends,* who were willing to put themselves on record, and that there is no testimony of a contrary kind except an early slur by a literary rival. If he had enemies, as he must have done, they lacked either the occasion or the zeal or the good luck to leave impeachments for posterity.

There he stands, then, distinct in outline but not in differentiating detail, almost a copybook figure of *Genus humanum* or "Everyman." The utility of this neutral outline I shall argue in conclusion. Shakespeare's outstanding trait, judging by the most recurrent words in early tributes, was simple affability—he was likable—but clearly this impression was derived mainly from his writings and might have prevailed no matter what he was like in the eyes of his wife, his maidservant, or his Maker. His lines were praised as "sugared," as "sweet," as "honey-flowing," his wit as of the "reigning" not "railing" sort, and so on. It may disturb those moderns who expatiate upon their grimness to learn that even his gravest plays struck the Elizabethans as "gentle." *Hamlet* itself was mentioned affectionately by Anthony Scoloker as another of "friendly Shakespeare's tragedies." [2] Our distrustful generation is suspicious of the affable, the friendly, the *good-natured,* which it is apt to view as stupid blandness or mercenary disguise, but we must reckon with the force of this early impression in the rise of Shakespeare's star.

"I loved the man," said Ben Jonson. [3] He was speaking of Shakespeare personally, but in a context suggesting that, in his mind, the idea of the poet and the idea of his poetry had coalesced, as they had done in the minds of others whose love, unlike Jonson's, had not stopped "this side idolatry." Dryden, born too late to know either Jonson or Shakespeare personally, said that he admired Jonson but loved Shakespeare.[4] We think we know what he meant. Jonson was the more "correct" writer by the critical standards which Dryden felt obliged to apply, but in Shakespeare was something unmeasurable by these standards. If asked to specify what that something is, we must inventory the homeliest kind of ingredients—the fun and good humor, the marks of generosity and fair-mindedness, the well of kindness implicit in the tenderness with which so many of his characters look upon so many others. Of course the veins of iron are there, so that by no feat of misunderstanding can we suspect panglossing, but the prevailing temper is benign. Our love of this writing seems repayment in kind. Bernard Shaw, at the height of his pose of hostility, gave his game away by calling it "endearing."[5] Only the most fanatic apostles of a "dark" Shakespeare can fail to perceive what is meant.

Now although Shakespeare was recognized as the best of English playwrights in his own age and during all but a few decades of the remaining seventeenth century, his standing was that of the popular entertainer rather than the literary artist. The sharp upward curve of his literary prestige came in the period 1680–1730 and was abetted, I believe, by the fact that his human warmth was welcome as relief from the Restoration chill. His works prospered in the new age of sensibility or of "sentimentality," which was at first no pejorative term. A fourth edition of the folio appeared in 1683, the first modern edition in 1709, and competing editions thereafter at ever-narrowing intervals. Nothing resembling this spate of publication had ever happened before to the works of a playwright. It means that there was a widening circle of readers, spontaneous readers uninfluenced as yet by curricular requirements or other forms of duress, and that more and more voices were communicating their enjoyment in tones of respect and affection. The voices, to be sure, were those of that minority which, in any age, reads literature, especially literature of the past, but when the minority speaks with respect and affection, the majority begins to listen. In the early decades of the eighteenth century Shakespeare was elevated to the place he has held ever since. Shakespeare became the "greatest."

It is a perilous thing to be the "greatest." Devotion to greatness is one thing, but devotion to the great and especially to the "greatest" can be something entirely different. Eminence rather than the reason for eminence can become the kindling power. Toadies crowd into the corner of the champion, and camp followers swarm in the wake of the conqueror. This is an unpleasant way to put it, and the phenomenon I am describing is not always disgusting. A charitable light is thrown upon it when we reflect that, regardless of their capacity to admire particular persons and things, all people need something to admire. Moreover, in matters of taste, hypocrisy is not only a tribute to virtue but sometimes its first phase; perhaps, in more instances than we are willing to concede, true appreciation follows upon initial pretense. The only point I am making is that, with the coming of Shakespeare's overwhelming fame, a new and imponderable factor began to operate in conceptions of him.

It may be that readers possessed the least distorted view of Shakespeare the man before any biography of him was written. The prefatory matter in the folios supplied his name, his portrait, and the obliquely imparted information that he was a native of Stratford who had become an actor in London. Readers could proceed on the comfortable assumption that the plays were written by a human being, while the plays themselves were suggesting that he was a human being of the more human kind. His earliest admirers were willing

6

to settle for this, as some are willing still. But in the dazzled eye of general posterity this simple image has been displaced by afterimages—the three most persistent of which I shall describe in succession: Shakespeare the enshrined, Shakespeare the socialite, and Shakespeare the penitent pilgrim.

In the early eighteenth century, at the same time that he was becoming discernible as an all-time literary winner, the first sketches of Shakespeare's life appeared in print; and devotion to him began to carry over into devotion to his town of Stratford, to the house on Henley Street formerly owned by his family, to the mulberry tree at New Place which he allegedly had planted, to thousands of snuffboxes and other trinkets carved from the inexhaustible wood of that mulberry tree, to bits of stone chipped from his last resting place, to countless rings, rapiers, gloves, and other garments certified to have touched his sacred form, and to hundreds of faked portraits. So far as these objects were valued in association with an idea, it was the idea of the sage or wisdom-bringer, but the idea was solvent in the magic. For an ever-increasing number the poet was ceasing to be a cherished idea and was becoming himself an object safely enshrined. At the present day a number of the Shakespeare centers include a reliquary. The Houghton Library at Harvard possessed hundreds of Shakespeare icons, bequeathed by devoted collectors, until a few years ago when it disposed of them en masse—further evidence, perhaps, of the hostility to religious feeling allegedly rampant at Cambridge.

Needless to say, Shakespeare's contemporaries would have been bewildered by the traffic in relics. Whether or not they loved the man, they certainly indulged in no rituals of worship. The hard fact is that not a single person among them seems to have preserved a single material object because it was associated with him. Not a letter, not a picture, not a personal possession—not even one of those mourning rings mentioned in his last testament. The only surviving tokens of sentiment are his funeral monument, no doubt commissioned by his family, and the First Folio of his plays, sponsored by his fellow actors and the stationers of London as one part memorial and nine parts commercial venture. The other objects are all spurious. The capital shrine is Stratford, England. We should acknowledge that it has stood up with more dignity than might have been expected under its crushing burden of honor. It is the *unofficial* Stratfordians who now, as in the past, engage in antics only slightly less ludicrous than those of the anti-Stratfordians, Baconian or otherwise. In recent years the Stratfordians and anti-Stratfordians, through "action" committees and reaction committees, have competed in their eagerness to dig up Shakespeare's bones. Totemism extends even to editions of his works—the "de luxe" editions brimming with irrelevant plates and other forms of illumination, minuscule editions in microscopic print, or their opposite in volumes so huge that a single man can scarcely lift one. Obviously these function as votary emblems rather than as books to be read. One regrets to say that ordinary editions sometimes function in the same way.

All of this is relatively harmless—certainly the least insidious form of idolatry. We may enjoy visiting the reliquaries as depositories of the curious; and libraries would be deprived of some of their wonder if purged of the queer editions. There does indeed seem to be some mystical power in the name "Stratford" since theaters come into being in the towns so named. Surely devotion to Shakespeare as secular saint is preferable to devotion to Bacon or Oxford as god. This latter is a cult of a different order which I have already treated once (in "Shakespeare as Culture Hero," below), and once is perhaps too often. Visiting shrines is not necessarily confined to those who limit their devotion to such an exercise.

We have all made our pilgrimages. In 1817 John Keats made his to Stratford, and, according to his companion, his enjoyment was of "that genuine, quiet kind which was a part of his gentle nature; deeply feeling what he truly enjoyed but saying little." Bailey tells how, at the Birthplace, they added their names "to the 'numbers numberless' of those which literally blackened the walls; and if those walls have not been washed, or our names washed out to find places for some others, they will still remain together upon that truly honored wall of a small low attic apartment." [6] The walls have indeed been "washed," and perhaps we betray our own share of superstition as we wish that the name of Keats had been permitted to stay. Charles Dickens, although happy that the private life of Shakespeare had resisted invasion and that the ghouls had not yet got his skull into the "phrenological shop-windows," was nevertheless active in the movement to preserve the "Birthplace." The attitude of Keats and Dickens seems to me preferable to that of Henry James, who because he was conscious of the spuriousness of the Shakespeare relics became darkly suspicious that Shakespeare himself was spurious.

Those most disdainful of the Stratford pilgrims prove to be members of a rival sect. Let me turn now from a foible of the masses to a foible of the classes—the social aggrandizement of Shakespeare. Not everyone has been moved by that "small low attic apartment" visited so lovingly by Keats. In 1769 the genteel world of London descended upon Stratford for the Garrick Shakespeare Jubilee. They found a small country town, much like other country towns, where, if the rain rained (as it did, in torrents), the streets grew very muddy. The buildings associated with the bard had not at that time had their faces lifted, and they proved to be far from elegant. The throng, however, was good-natured, and although they may secretly have wished that Shakespeare had been born at Bath, where the tourist accommodations were better, they were willing to accept Stratford as the proper kind of setting for the beginning of a Dick Whittington story—of the poor boy who made good. In fact the eighteenth century cult of genius, which induced learned men to look hopefully for sparks of poetic fire in the givings-forth of rural blacksmiths and illiterate washerwomen, may have lent to the mire of Henley Street even a certain glamor.

But as biographical research progressed, through the industry of men like Edmond Malone, it became more and more evident that the notion of Shakespeare as apotheosized "poor boy" or isolated genius simply would not do. Each new piece of evidence placed him more and more firmly within a bourgeois setting. Most of the biographers, and especially the critics of the biographers, were themselves gentry. They could have accepted without discomfort the idea of a Shakespeare risen from the peasantry like Joan of Arc, but not as a member of the lower middle class. Signs of embarrassment begin to appear, at first taking the form of mockery at the findings of Malone, which were stigmatized as "trivial." A note of defensiveness or rueful amusement begins to sound in the voices of gentlemen scholars, even enthusiasts like Halliwell-Phillipps. One can imagine their inner communings: why, after all, did the Orpheus of England have to be born over a *shop*? or hoard in his cellar barrels of *malt*? or sue anyone for the pitiful sum of thirty-five *shillings*? or—God save the mark!—have to mention in his will such a deplorable object as a *second-best bed*? Moreover, Shakespeare had been nurtured by no one's alma mater, and to the proud sons of Oxford and Cambridge the efficacy of the Stratford grammar school seemed small consolation. One is reminded of the American preparatory school student who left a history class in a state of shock upon learning that

Lincoln had failed not only to make a fraternity but even to go to college.

The unease had been mounting for some years before Sidney Lee's *Life of William Shakespeare* appeared in 1898. Readers found that Lee had not only accepted the fact of the poet's bourgeois background and practical habits but had even done so with a certain relish, asserting at one point (truly with some oversimplification) that Shakespeare's "literary attainments and successes were chiefly valued as serving the prosaic end of making a permanent provision for himself and his daughters."[7] Charges were made that Lee had *traduced* Shakespeare. As late as 1932 John Dover Wilson produced his own biographical sketch, *The Essential Shakespeare,* with the avowed intent of fumigating the poet from the clinging scent of Lee. He began by saying that Lee must have formed his conception of Shakespeare from gazing too long at his bust in Holy Trinity Church. He then proceeded to ridicule the bust. In the process of saying much about images false and true, he employed some rather disturbing imagery—for instance, that the Stratford bust bears less resemblance to a poet than to a "self-satisfied pork-butcher."[8] Now we can be reasonably sure that Professor Wilson, who we must remember is a gifted scholar, had made no systematic study of the faces of pork-butchers, self-satisfied or otherwise, and that if he had done so he might have found them, since he is also a genial and humane man, not uniformly repugnant. His choice of epithet may have been unconsciously dictated by a latent dissatisfaction with the Shakespeare family trade, which was not altogether distinguishable from that of the butcher. In any case, he chose as the frontispiece of his own biography the portrait of a youth of Shakespeare's era, admittedly not identifiable as the poet, but very handsome in a genteel sort of way.

The Stratford bust and the folio engraving are the only portraits of Shakespeare with a claim to authenticity, and it must be granted that both are lacking in that human warmth associated with him. There is no sparkle in the eye of the bust, and the domelike brow of the engraving looks capacious but unendearing. We must remember, however, that these portraits are themselves afterimages, fashioned several years after the subject's death, with the possible aid of a life mask, the sole object of the makers having been an effect of dignity and acumen. We must remember, too, that the faces of poets may sometimes appear less poetic than their souls, as witness some living examples. The souls of poets, like our own, must wear the muddy vesture of decay, and although I should like to think that Shakespeare's eyes were indeed "light hazel with spots like gold-dust," as maintained by the Comtesse de Chambrun,[9] I am forced to testify that her evidence leaves something to be desired. The face of Keats the man was ideally suitable for Keats the poet, but not his five-foot stature—Keats should have been tall as Apollo.

The hostility aroused by Lee's biography reflects the fear, endemic in polite circles, that Shakespeare was of the tribe of Johnny-come-latelies or pushing "townies." Many wish to believe that, whatever his origins, he could have mingled on easy terms with the Elizabethan nobility; and would have him not only a natural gentleman, as we can easily imagine, but also a naturalized aristocrat, a concept much more mystical. Most of the many modern biographies brim with wishful thinking. Even the most slender evidence of the poet's association with the socially elite is exploited to the hilt. His troupe (like all theatrical troupes) had as nominal patron a member of the nobility or royal family, and this font of purple blood becomes the personal patron of Shakespeare (although not of other members of his troupe or the members of other troupes). The "friend" in the sonnets is assumed to be a youth of noble birth, but in their unco-operative way the sonnets never say so, and the "dark mistress" is assumed to be, at least technically, a *lady,* although the sonnets never say that either. By a process of simple repetition Southampton the dedicatee has become Southampton the "patron," and Shakespeare's mastery of the conventional dedicatory style has fanned up belief in a "mutual flame." In fact it has been "proved," or at least judged "sensible" to believe, that this earl and this actor, unlike any other earl and actor of any conceivable Elizabethan world, were on chiding terms with each other, corresponded in sonnets (preserving copies in chronological order), and after a three or four year season of *Schwärmerei* "broke up" less in anger than in sorrow. If it is not true, it is the silliest fiction ever to win acceptance.

Every available lord has been nominated as the true author of Shakespeare's works, and to conclude therefore that, whoever the author, it must have been *some* lord strikes me as very defective reasoning, but this is how the unwary mind works. Several different lords have been advocated anew this year as the "friend" of the sonnets, and one has the right to conclude that the so-called evidence in each case must be something less than conclusive. Vociferous repetition proves nothing except the emotional needs of the disputants. It is all part of a continuing tradition: by hook or by crook the lordliness of the lords is made to rub off on the householder of Stratford and actor of London.

But as he lay dying and instructed his executors, no recollection of noble intimates seems to have passed through Shakespeare's mind. Here the sentimental provisions of the will are significant even if the practical ones are not. There are token bequests for Burbage, Hemming, and Condell, the surviving members of his old acting troupe; for Thomas Combe and other small Warwickshire landowners like himself; and for members of his family, including his maligned wife, Anne. This evidence is in agreement with all the rest. There is not a shred of proof that Shakespeare was ever intimate or socially familiar with anyone except members of his own class: his fellow actors and writers in London, his Stratford neighbors, and his kinsmen and kinsmen-in-law. Every historical probability argues that he was not. There is not a shred of proof that he ever received so much as a shilling from a lord as a gift, although he was probably paid by Southampton for his dedications, or even a free dinner in a lordly household, although a seat at the servants' table would have been a customary perquisite when his troupe made a professional visit. Unlike Jonson, Shakespeare never received a lucrative commission for an entertainment or masque at a noble or royal household. The legend that he received from Southampton the preposterously large sum of £1000 first appeared in print a hundred years after his death and marks a beginning of that effort I am tracing to create for him noble associations. The two most publicized biographies of the quadricentennial year fairly bristle with noble lords, featured in elegant illustrations and in shrill cries of "Eureka." The true mystery is how they got there.

It would be hypocritical of us, even in America where they are unconstitutional, to sneer at lords. Most of us would admit that if we had been Elizabethans we would prefer to have been lords. One is reminded of John Bunyan's musings, recorded in *Grace Abounding,* that if he had to go to hell, as seemed to him probable, he hoped he might be a devil and not one of the mere sinners whom they tortured. If we could not have been lords, we would like to have had access to their tables and cellars, and the run of their libraries, spacious halls, and green pleasances. Stephen Leacock's declaration that he liked to mix with the rich because he liked the things they mix expresses a healthy attitude, but it is not the attitude of those who have thrust Shakespeare into a lordly Elysium. The benefits accruing to him appear to be of a more spiritual order, in some indefinable way adding cubits unto his stature. But if we reflect for a moment, we must realize that, compared with great accomplishers, especially artistic geniuses, lords in every age come as thick as currants in a bun. If one were thinking of what a privilege it would have been for Southampton, Essex, Pembroke, or the like to link arms with Shakespeare, and were acting on the generous impulse to let them do so, it would be a different matter, but these worthies probably missed their chance and it is too late to help them now. On the other hand, if one loves Shakespeare the better the higher company he keeps, one should listen to Cordelia's France,

> Love's not love
> When it is mingled with regards that stand
> Aloof from the entire point.

Shakespeare himself valued social position, and did what he could to raise that of his family—buying land, entailing his estate, and securing a coat of arms for his father so that he himself might almost be a "gentleman born"—but this snobbery, to call it such, was owing partly to prudence, partly to modesty: he did not realize the extent to which he had otherwise dignified his name, what larger titles he could claim.

I turn now to the afterimage which has exercised the greatest influence upon criticism—that of Shakespeare the penitent pilgrim. After scholars had succeeded in placing the plays in a tentative chronological order, there followed a tendency to use them as biographical stepping stones. After reading them in order of composition, one could make surmises about the author's changing moods, his elation over success, his distress at failure, his ambivalent feelings toward the Essex rebellion, the psychic crisis induced by the death of his father, and so on. The most amazing fruits of this effort have been articles in the psychoanalytical journals, which make the thesis of Freud and Jones about the Oedipal inspiration of *Hamlet* seem stodgily old-fashioned. Analysts have pointed to episodes in the lives of Shakespeare's mother, sisters, and daughters in conjunction with "symptoms" revealed in his plays to demonstrate the release of every known variety of suppressed incestuous emotion, invisible to the lay eye but quite perspicuous to that of the psychoscientist. We need not linger with this harrowing chronicle, since it is only the grotesque shadow of another.

The basic chronicle took primitive form in 1878 when Edward Dowden's *Shakespeare Primer* offered its famous formulation: "In the Workshop . . . In the World . . . Out of the Depths . . . On the Heights." This fed, in a moderate way, the natural craving for some kind of dramatic life history, or at least some principle of organization tying together detached literary and biographical facts. The reading of the plays as autobiography was stimulated, until gradually the book which in 1623 had been called *Master William Shakespeare's Comedies, Histories, and Tragedies* was transformed into another book, which might well be called "The Poet-Pilgrim's Progress." Even the soundest critics and scholars have added a touch here and there to this revision. Sir Edmund Chambers, who of all Shakespeareans commands my greatest respect and gratitude, became himself something of a Bunyan when he left facts and problems and let his imagination range in criticism. Professor John Dover Wilson's natural flair for the dramatic has made him a notable contributor; and in such works as Sean O'Laughlin's and Kenneth Muir's *Voyage to Illyria* we are conducted upon some curious side excursions.

In outline the tale goes something like this. Youth, callow and even apish, is projected in the early histories and farces, commendable in their way, but showing scarcely enough sign of the poet's personal agony to keep them interesting. Excitement picks up when we slip in among the plays the presumed Story of the Sonnets, Shakespeare's presumed involvement in the cause of the Earl of Essex, and his presumed mental and physical crisis after the turn of the century. Shakespeare the Pilgrim passes from the City of Destruction, escaping with Prince Hal from the seductive clutches of Falstaff, and then, whether through the private misconduct of a dark lady or the public misconduct of a light nobleman, finds himself in the Valley of Humiliation. He sojourns with the Giant Despair at Doubting Castle (*Hamlet*), struggles through the Slough of Despond (the "dark" comedies), then passes through the Valley of the Shadow of Death (the great tragedies), wrestling in *King Lear* with the fiend Apollyon. The way then brightens in the romances. It is not clear when the Pilgrim crosses the Delectable Mountains (unless represented by the rocky terrain of *Cymbeline*), but there is no doubt about when he reaches Beulah-land. It is located on the seacoast of Bohemia, and the time of arrival, dramatically abrupt, is the beginning of the fourth act of *The Winter's Tale*. In Beulah-land the

Air was very sweet and pleasant, . . . Yea, here [he] heard continually the singing of Birds, and saw every day the flowers appear in the earth: and heard voices of the Turtle in the Land. In this Countrey the Sun shineth night and day; wherefore this was beyond the Valley of the shadow of death, and also out of the reach of the Giant Despair; neither could [he] from this place so much as see Doubting-Castle.[10]

We are given by Wilson a final glimpse of the Pilgrim in the holy hush of *The Tempest*—"no prophet upon the heights, but a penitent on his knees."[11]

To remark that the penitent rises from his knees at least long enough to compose a ribald ditty about the nautical aversions of Kate proves irresistible, but to submit to pure mockery the Bunyanesque conception of Shakespeare's career would be neither gracious nor fair, since most of us have been influenced by it somewhat and there are reasons why we should be. The shadow of the valley of death truly does lie upon the great tragedies, and the description of Beulah-land truly does suggest the coast where the soul-healing Perdita is found. But we must ask at last just why the life of Shakespeare in particular should be seen as a salvation story: what were his known sins? Surely those who picture him on his knees at forty-seven are not thinking of his precipitancy with Anne Hathaway at eighteen? or the occasion when he was tardy in paying his taxes? or even his unpoetic insistence that money due him be paid? Of course there is his "affair" with the dark mistress, but this sin merges imperceptibly into that of his murdering King Duncan since its imaginative coefficient remains undetermined. Shakespeare seems to have spent most of his adult life writing and acting in plays, and I suspect that the idea of his redemption (at retirement) is not wholly unrelated to the age-old suspicion of the theater as the vestibule of hell. If we ask what Shakespeare in particular had to repent, perhaps we must answer that it was writing all of his plays except *The Tempest*. Factual inconsistencies appear in the reconstruction of his life from his works even in its least elaborated form. For instance, the event which we may reasonably guess was the most tragic in his life, the death of his only son Hamnet in 1596, occurred at the inception of his alleged "joyous period," while his "tragic period," when he has been pictured as despondent to the verge of madness, proves synchronous with his busiest concern with Warwickshire real estate.

Let me attempt a little summing up before proffering my message. We must wish with Burke to refrain from indicting a whole people, and the three "afterimages" I have described are too widely current to be dismissed with contempt. Something may be said for all of them, and the best is that, in the way of afterimages, they alter coloration rather than shape or size. Their effect is not to *diminish* Shakespeare. In this respect they compare well with visions of the egocentric sects. We must remember that Shakespeare has been pictured as a subversive by the subversives, a deviate by the deviates, and so on—especially, in our own obsessed age, as a satyr by the satyrs, or rather by the latter's literary fetches who, whether for our amusement, admiration, or envy, exhibit their inky ejaculations. The three commonest afterimages are indubitably more generous. The mass homage to Shakespeare-reliquiae attests a guileless faith that he was the best of his kind, whatever that kind may have been; the conferring upon him of the society of lords is a free gift of status, which we now hear is the thing that men most desire; and the assumption that he was a sinner is no more than a necessary adjunct to the kind assumption that he at last found grace. Most men suspect, toward the end, that their lives have been misspent, and they may be right in assuming that Shakespeare was similarly obsessed; in any case they are willing to strike the bargain with Prospero—

> As you from crimes would pardoned be,
> Let your indulgence set me free.

The true defect of the afterimages, apart from their fictive quality, is that they displace a conception at once less vulnerable and more useful. The veneration of relics makes Shakespeare seem terribly dead. His social elevation removes him somewhat from our own sphere. The interpretation of his works as autobiography reduces the universal to the particular. Some of the sonnets are among the greatest poems in the language, and to insist that they were inspired by a crush on this person or that does violence to our instincts. Dramatic characters shrink when identified as particular friends, enemies, or political candidates of the artist; we prefer Hamlet as Hamlet to Hamlet as the Earl of Essex. And the treatment of plays as episodes in a salvation story spells critical disintegration: if this early comedy is an indiscreet "experiment," this middle tragedy a "symptom," this late romance a "testament," where are the works of art?

The contrived biographical formulations make us do something which biographical documents leave us free not to do. The actual records, as I have said, preserve a neutrality which seems almost a calculated gift of destiny. Was his an impetuous love-marriage? We must hesitate to say so, but it was surely no marriage of convenience. Did he have a good or a poor formal education? There is evidence on both sides. Was the "story" of the sonnets truth or fiction? The only ones rash enough to answer this question are those who are rash enough to believe that the sonnets tell us what the "story" is. And so it goes. We know that Shakespeare was a particular man, but we do not really know what particular kind of man. And why should this be fortunate? It is so because he is important to us in other than his private capacity. He belongs to all, and not to those alone who have had or think they have had peeps behind the curtain. About him we know neither too much nor too little. In the case of many authors we unhappily know too much. In the case of only a few does our appreciation increase as our knowledge of their private lives becomes more detailed. It does so in the case of Samuel Johnson and John Keats. I would add to this number Charles Dickens, but not everyone would agree. And there is the point. As Dickens himself observed, there is in the case of Shakespeare no true room for disagreement; he is, said Dickens, a "fine mystery." We know if we are honest-minded that all we can say is that "He was a man."

But, curious as it seems, these are in Shakespeare's own lexicon the words of highest praise. "'A was a man, take him for all in all"—this is Prince Hamlet's epitaph for his father, and we all remember Antony's: "This was a man." Pascal, who was born in the year of the First Folio, still sees the refulgent image of man as man: "People should not be able to say of anyone that he is a mathematician, or a preacher, or an eloquent man, but that he is a *man*. Only this universal quality pleases me." [12] I hope I am becoming clear. Shakespeare's life records, like his works, allow us to contemplate the "universal quality," and if we have what Keats called "negative capability" we will accept the uncertainty about particulars with gratitude. Surely we are under no obligation to accept the dusty answers evoked by a lust for certainty.

The names of Dickens and Keats have been haunting me, possibly because I think that an amalgam of their talents would have given us another Shakespeare. It was Keats who saw the advantage of the image of Shakespeare as man, rather than as this or that kind of man. He saw that the life of Shakespeare was an allegorical journey of another kind from that of Bunyan's Christian. In a letter to his brother in America in 1819 he said,

A Man's life of any worth is a continual allegory—and very few eyes can see the Mystery of his life—a life like the scriptures, figurative—which such people can no more make out than they can the hebrew Bible. Lord Byron cuts a figure—but he is not figurative—Shakespeare led a life of Allegory; his works are the comments on it. [13]

What Keats is saying is that Shakespeare's significant life was not the literal one of specific personal experience, but the allegorical one of which his plays are the expression. Those who strive to individualize him by picturing the woebegone lover, the politician manqué, or whatever it may be are making him, like Lord Byron, "cut a figure," and are reducing his "figurative," his large allegorical, significance. Shakespeare may best be thought about as Everyman, and his biography as the life's journey of Everyman. His nature was such that the important episodes in that life's journey were not his experiences as self but his experiences as Man. I do not believe that this image is so "impersonal" that it cancels out even those impressions which I described as those of his first admirers—of a person friendly, humorous, kind. Surely this is what it means truly to be a man. Everyman is not average man, whatever that may be, but the abstract of what makes men men. The only one fitted for the allegorical journey of Everyman, of man as man, would be one of ourselves at our best.

2 THE MYTH OF PERFECTION

*U*NTIL that halcyon day when we shall all see eye to eye, the best we can do is exchange provisional maps sketched from particular points of vantage. One of the things which I seem to see is the protean character of Shakespeare idolatry as it has emerged in various ages—in forms as varied (and increasingly formidable) as an eighteenth-century textual emendation, a nineteenth-century treatise on the playwright's legal lore, and a twentieth-century volume of "interpretive" criticism.

It may seem a far cry from the militant Baconian or Oxfordian to the obscure eighteenth-century don demonstrating Shakespeare's knowledge of Greek, or the mild nineteenth-century naturalist demonstrating his knowledge of botany, but there is a connection both practical and theoretic. The scholar who "proves" that the author was a scholar provides footing for the mythmaker who "proves" that he could not have been a non-university man. This is the practical connection. The theoretic is more interesting. It may be touching to observe the naturalist bestowing upon his revered fellow countryman, who he stoutly maintains was yeoman born and bred, all his own specialized knowledge of Warwickshire flora and fauna, but what if Shakespeare actually possessed no such knowledge? could even err on occasion about the color of a wild-flower of the source of its perfume? Apparently he knew that snakes cast their enameled skins, but it is doubtful if he know how they injected their venom. He surely knew that toads bore no precious jewels in their heads, but he may have believed them to be poisonous as well as ugly; whether he knew how they "engendered" is a moot point. What the enthusiastic naturalist has done, although it seems cruel to say so, is to indulge in a form of idolatry, by creating a god in his own image.

So with the various musicians, sailors, soldiers, doctors, and others, especially lawyers, who have brought their offerings to the shrine, and have fostered the idea that Shakespeare not only knew and loved music, as he truly did, but could take down and reassemble a spinet (if he did not invent the instrument) as well as navigate a ship, command an army, and perform a frontal lobotomy, while his exhaustive knowledge of the law might have ruptured even the capacious brain of the Lord Chief Justice. Of course none of these things are true, since the plays and poems, in indicating that their author was well informed—an excellent observer, especially of nature—are also indicating that he possessed specialized knowledge of nothing, except how to write plays and poems. The notion of his prodigious "knowledge" is attributable in part to his skill as an illusionist. Anyone who has written even a routine piece of fiction is aware of the necessity of faking—of using strategically his bits of technical knowledge so that his lawyers will seem like lawyers, his doctors doctors, his priests priests, and so on. The bits expand in the reader's imagination into a comprehensive body of knowledge, undefined in the layman's but specialized in the specialist's, provided the character to whom they are attached is convincing. The naive response is to identify the presumed knowledge of the characters with the actual knowledge of the author, when often, in such cases, the part of the iceberg of knowledge which shows is the only part which exists. But Shakespeare's more than routine skill in deception fails to account in full for the myth of his omniscience. The myth derives from and contributes to an embracing myth. Had he not already assumed superhuman proportions in their minds, the specialists would have noted his misses as well as hits in their fields of competence, and would not have collaborated in making him still more superhuman by endowing him with specialized knowledge of all the specialties.

My primary concern is with the effect of *mythos* upon current Shakespearean criticism. The approach may seem devious, but myths mature slowly, and the way that ancient editors looked at single words throws light on the way that modern critics look at whole plays. It is common knowledge that some of the eighteenth-century editors blamed every defect in the texts upon the interpolation of actors, the incompetence of scribes and printers, and the villainy of former editors. Positing an original composition "worthy" of Shakespeare, they corrected the grammar, regularized the meter, improved the diction, and straightened out classical, geographical, and other allusions. This is a stale subject, and I do not wish to make capital of the misdemeanors of "bad" editors. I shall cite the respectable ones, as later I shall refer in general to respectable critics. Lewis Theobald was one of the best. In preparing his edition of 1733, he was confronted by the following in the Folio text of *Measure for Measure:*

> But this new Gouernor
> Awakes me all the inrolled penalties
> Which haue (like vn-scowr'd Armor) hung by th' wall
> So long, that ninteene Zodiacks haue gone round,
> And none of them beene worne; . . .

Thus Claudio in I.iii. But in the very next scene, less than fifty lines later, the Duke says,

> We haue strict Statutes, and most biting Laws,
> (The needfull bits and curbes to headstrong weedes,)
> Which for this fourteene yeares, we haue let slip, . . .

Whether "weedes" had better be emended to "steeds" or "wills" and "slip" to "sleep" are debatable points with which we need not linger (although editors have properly done so) except to observe that two questionable readings in three lines throw some suspicion upon the accuracy of the Folio at this point. The glaring discrepancy is between the Duke's "fourteene" and Claudio's "ninteene." Says Theobald in reference to it, "For *fourteen* I have made no Scruple to replace *nineteen*. . . . The Author could not so disagree with himself in so narrow a Compass." In the words *could not* (which should have been *probably did not*) we detect just a hint of the myth of perfection. Theobald adds, "The Numbers must have been wrote in Figures, and so mistaken. . . ."[1] When we understand what this acute editor was implying—that if the author's script contained roman numerals, his *xix* might easily have been mistaken by a scribe or compositor for *xiv*—we can appreciate the cogency of his reasoning.

But there is a catch in it. If *xix* might easily have been mistaken for *xiv*, then *xiv* might just as easily have been mistaken for *xix*, so that it may be Claudio's figure which needs correction. Peter Whalley raised the issue in his own way, by saying, with a true-born Englishman's respect for rank, which he assumed that Shakespeare shared, "I am disposed to take the Duke's words." Here there is more than a hint of the myth of perfection, because the grounds are not graphic plausibility but simply "Shakespearean" propriety. Finally Edmond Malone cut the knot by asserting that both the "nineteen" and "fourteen" should stand: "Claudio would naturally represent the period during which the law had not been put in practice greater than it was."[2] Now here, although Malone was neither idolatrous nor an inferior editor, by the standards of his day, we have the myth of perfection full-blown. A blemish has been rationalized into a beauty, a discrepancy into a subtlety, a numerical error into a "touch of nature."

In 1863 the Cambridge editors stated a good general principle by which the "nineteen-fourteen" dilemma might be resolved: "If [a] defect can be made good in more ways than one equally plausible, or, at least, equally probable, we have registered but not adopted these improvements, and the reader is intended to make his own selection out of the notes." [3] In all modern editions the "nineteen-fourteen" discrepancy is permitted to stand, but usually there is no note, and we do not know whether it is for Malone's reason, or for the Cambridge editors' reason—or for a reason elsewhere given by Malone himself (". . . our author is often incorrect in the computation of time") [4] and endorsed by Dover Wilson ("The discrepancy may well be Shakespeare's"). [5] This is one of the thousands of tiny bones which faintly rattle in the textual closet. In 1905 H. C. Hart reverted to the position of Whalley: ". . . his [the Duke's] word must, of course, be accepted." [6] About Malone's explanation, that people naturally exaggerate figures in the direction of their desires, Hart asks plaintively, "Is this convincing?" We must admit that it is not. But (disregarding the possibility that Shakespeare was cryptically predicting the advent of the First World War) we may suggest that the Duke, who is still a bachelor and hence relatively young, only succeeded to the dukedom fourteen years before, at which time the law had already lain dormant for five years, so that Claudio's "nineteen" and his "fourteen" are both literally correct. Is this convincing? No.

The trouble with the type of explanation based upon a presumed psychological or factual consistency is that, in laying one ghost, it raises thousands more. When Romeo sees Juliet across a crowded room and asks a servant who she is, we get:

> *Servant.*   I know not, sir.
> *Romeo.* O, she doth teach the torches to burn bright.

One can imagine a reader (more interested in hard facts than in love) being more moved by the servant's line than by

Romeo's: "Why this is preposterous! A lovely heiress, and the only child of the house, and yet this servant does not even know who she is!" In which case, following Malone's example, we would have to suggest that this particular servant must be part-time help, or that since Juliet is only fourteen years old come Lammastide, she has been drilled not to speak to strangers and the servants not to give out information.

In all the plays of Shakespeare there are discrepancies—real ones, not conventional ones like the convenient ignorance of the Capulet servant. At one point in *The Merchant of Venice* all the early texts read "Mantua" where clearly the right place is "Padua." A kind of territorial restitution is made in *The Taming of the Shrew* where the Folio reads "Padua" when clearly the right place is "Mantua" (or "Pisa"). In the first scene of *The Merry Wives of Windsor* the first name of Master Page is "Thomas," but thereafter it becomes "George." Names can change in whole as well as in part. In *Measure for Measure* the character designated simply as "Clown" in the speech prefixes is first addressed as "Thomas Tapster," but when his name is formally demanded of him, it proves to be "Pompey Bum." (In *King John* it is a monarch's name which fluctuates, not just a lowly pimp's.) Characters can change their physical characteristics. In *As You Like It* Celia is "taller" than Rosalind until it is time for them to assume disguises, whereupon Rosalind becomes taller than Celia. Characters can evaporate completely—or never really materialize. Several are mentioned in the original stage directions of *2 Henry IV* who are given nothing to do or say. The most remarkable instance of this kind is the strange case of Hero's mother. Let me quote the delightful comment of Sir Edmund Chambers: "Leonato is accompanied by 'Innogen his wife' at the beginning of *Much Ado About Nothing*. She recurs in one later scene, but has not a word throughout the play. A Lady, whose daughter is successively betrothed, defamed, repudiated before the altar, taken for dead, and restored to life, ought not to be a mute. It is not motherly." [7]

The editor of the fine New Variorum text of 2 *Henry IV* speaks of the silent and superfluous characters whom Shakespeare "forgot to write a part for." [8] In reference to Innogen in *Much Ado About Nothing* Chambers speaks of the possibility of abridgment, and then asks, "But did Shakespeare sometimes write initial entries before he had thought out the dialogue, and omit through carelessness to correct them by eliminating characters for whom he had found nothing to say, and ought to have found something to say, if they were to be on the stage at all?" [9] Professor Shaaber's word "forgot" and Sir Edmund's word "carelessness" would have offended the piety of some of their predecessors. Modern editors are aware that Shakespeare cannot be wholly exonerated of responsibility for the many imperfections which appear in the texts, even though they may alter "Mantua" to "Padua" (or "Padua" to "Mantua"), "Thomas" to "George," and ruthlessly delete "Innogen." If they diminish a "taller" Celia to a "smaller" Celia, at least they do not argue that Rosalind grew in stature when she fell in love. I have given only a meager sampling of the many discrepancies that cannot be attributed to any deep and dark design. Since the eighteenth century, the myth of perfection has steadily waned among textual scholars, but this does not mean that the myth has been on the wane.

At the beginning of *A Midsummer Night's Dream* Theseus and Hippolyta reiterate the fact that *four* days must intervene before their nuptials, but that happy event ensues in two. In 1879 F. Gard Fleay tackled this problem [10] after his contemporaries had wrestled with the wayward behavior of time in the other plays and had devised schedules to their satisfaction. He gained one day by coolly asserting the existence of a twenty-four-hour interval in the first scene, and a second day by suggesting that the sleep of the lovers in the wood endured for twenty-four hours. Their peculiar torpor he explained as follows: the nuptials take place on a May Day, the play was performed in 1592, and in 1592 the day before May Day was a Sunday. The reasoning is not wholly perspicuous; presumably we must deduce that on Sundays even bivouacking lovers sleep late, or that since Sunday-marriages were interdicted, sleeping out the day was the only thing Shakespeare could find for them to do.

Fleay's effort is an extreme example of nineteenth-century rationalizations. The eighteenth-century sophisticators of the text were scolded by the nineteenth-century rationalizers, at the same time that the latter were imitating them. Idolatry was not falling into decay; it was rebuilding on higher ground. Malone's comment on Claudio's "nineteen" really links him with the romantic critics rather than with the "bad" editors like Pope, Warburton, and Hanmer. These critics, from Morgann to Bradley, have been sufficiently reproved for their "character mongering" and "psychologizing" to spare me the task of illustrating their tactics. Of course the discussion of characters and psychology is not in itself inappropriate in commentary on dramatic works, and the charge against the "romantics," so far as it is valid, means only that they carried this kind of commentary beyond the point where it is either valid or relevant. The assumption of perfection, of a "true-to-life" consistency, led to hypothetical constructions, perhaps consistent with themselves, but only coincidentally related to Shakespeare's plays. Reference was made to the childhood of the characters, their behavior off-stage, and their private domestic arrangements, for instance the present whereabouts of the child whom Lady Macbeth has borne and suckled. As with the earlier editors, so with these extratextual critics, the scent of incense is strongest in the vicinity of the least able.

In the twentieth century the rationalizers have been succeeded by the exegetes, who again imitate as they scold; but no longer can we say that the scent of incense is strongest in the vicinity of the least able. A really ominous progression has occurred. It is now the major Shakespearean critics who serve the myth of perfection. Let me pause for a definition. The mark of idolatry is not excessive enthusiasm, a rapturous tone, the use of superlatives, the invention of new terms of praise in ecstatic prose or verse. Were such the case, Ben Jonson would qualify as a Shakespeare idolater; he is one of the few, after all, who have equated the poet with actual gods—"like Apollo . . . like a Mercury." The mark of idolatry is the assumption that because the plays are excellent, they are excellent in every way—in a word that they are *perfect*— with the perfection which is finally assumed so distinctly in the beholder's eyes, so exclusively *his* conception of perfection, that for the excellence they truly possess is substituted an excellence (if we may call it such) which they do not possess, and which might not even be proper to works of art as distinct from academic manuals, case histories, or social and ethical tractates. If this definition is tenable, as it seems to be in respect to the faulty past, we are in a parlous state because no longer, as in that past, are the major critics free.

Samuel Johnson was the major Shakespearean critic of the eighteenth century, and his freedom from idolatry need not be argued but taken as read. Samuel Coleridge was the major Shakespearean critic of the nineteenth century, and his *relative* freedom from idolatry, although it cannot be adequately argued in a paragraph, can be reasonably maintained if we admit the crucial distinction between extravagant praise and transmutation of the thing praised. I can only point out

that Coleridge's *Hamlet* criticism, which is his most idolatrous, is not his total Shakespearean criticism, and that his
statement (or, rather, the statement approximately his) that
"Assuredly, that criticism of Shakespeare will alone be genial
which is reverential"[11] is by no means a religious manifesto.
Quite often those very turns of phrase most suggestive of
idolatry to modern ears are evidence of the reverse. They are
most apt to occur when Coleridge is having honest doubts:
"It is too venturesome to charge a speech in Shakespeare
with want of truth to nature. And yet. . . ." (I, 104); whereupon he explains why a speech in *As You Like It* gives him
pause. He comments unhappily upon a speech in *Coriolanus*
and concludes, "I cherish the hope that I am mistaken, and,
becoming wiser, shall discover some profound excellence in
what I now appear to myself to detect an imperfection"
(I, 91). This sounds pious, indeed mealy-mouthed, but the
great point is that he had *not* discovered, had not *forced*
himself to discover, a "profound excellence" in what looked
like an "imperfection." And when he disliked a play he could
say so in round terms—to him *Measure for Measure* seemed
a "hateful" work.

By major critics I mean those most widely read and influen-
tial. It is hard to imagine the major Shakespearean critics of
the twentieth century being given pause by anything, or
failing to discover any exellence which they hope to find,
or—and this especially—viewing *Measure for Measure* as a
"hateful" work or, indeed, marred by a single flaw. The
recent history of this play illustrates perfectly the increasing
pervasiveness of the myth of perfection.

Let me return for a moment to the matter of the state of
Shakespeare's texts. Those who read the plays only in modern
editions are spared many annoyances but they are denied
many small revelations. The cumulative impact of the latter
can be considerable. After meeting in every play such in-

stances as the "Mantua" which should be "Padua," the "Thomas" who should be "George," and the ghost-like "Innogen" who should not be there at all, one draws new conclusions about the kind of material with which one is dealing. Granted that the great majority of the discrepancies are owing to scribal and printing errors (themselves eloquent of the disturbing fact that Shakespeare never found it worthwhile to oversee the printing and proofreading of a single play, including the "good" quarto of *Hamlet*), a residue still remain for which his habits of composition must be held accountable. It becomes evident to the secular-minded that he was capable of offhand improvisation, that he sometimes began a play without knowing how it was going to end, that he often failed to name characters until he was far along in the script, and that he just as often failed to clear away chips as he hewed to an emerging line. Celia's initial tallness may be a minor case in point. It would have been natural for him to visualize Rosalind as a pert little brunette like Hermia, Celia a willowy blonde like Helena, until he came to the point of disguising them as brother and sister, and absent-mindedly canceled the conception. This may not be what happened, but parallel discrepancies leave no doubt that it *could* have happened.

Shakespeare could even get hopelessly bogged down in his syntax, and yet let the snarled passage stand. Even in texts as good as that of *The Tempest,* or in dual texts with independent authority like those of *Hamlet,* where identical recurrence of certain passages performs an authenticating function, there are lines which should have been revised or "blotted." Notorious passages appear both in early plays like *The Comedy of Errors* and in late ones like *Cymbeline,* where no reasonable emendation can cure the incoherence or obscurity. Commentators must suggest a "missing line," or maintain a gloomy silence. The reader may wish to exercise himself by trying to parse (with the aid of Abbott) the following from the last scene in *Cymbeline:*

> The peece of tender Ayre, thy vertuous Daughter
> Which we call *Mollis Aer,* and *Mollis Aer*
> We terme it *Mulier;* which *Mulier* I diuine
> Is that most constant Wife, who euen now
> Answering the Letter of the Oracle,
> Vnknowne to you, vnsought, were clipt about
> With this most tender Aire.

Here the meaning is clear enough, but in similar cases it can only be guessed.

My intention, of course, is not to "debunk" Shakespeare. Surely we can tolerate the bad passages in view of others where an almost equally cavalier disregard for syntax accompanies magnificent effects. And there are indeed apparent discrepancies which are in fact subtleties, or at least the product of conscious artistic calculation. And plays retaining the debris of false starts, like *Much Ado About Nothing,* can turn out fine in the end. Nevertheless we must recognize that the merit in Shakespeare's plays does not extend to merit in every detail in them; and whether particular defects, in minor or major features, are attributable to Shakespeare himself or to accidents of transmission, the fact remains that they are there. Reliable conclusions cannot be drawn from unreliable or incomplete data. Disquisitions upon dramatic structure are worthless if based upon act divisions carelessly dubbed in by the publishers of the Folio; and ecstasies over the inspired placing of a colon are unrewarding if the colon represents not Shakespeare's "dramatic punctuation" but the bright idea of a printer's apprentice. If there are inconsistencies in things so conspicuous as the naming of persons and places, there can be inconsistencies in the choice of images, so that the plays cannot be treated as if they were machine-tooled mechanisms, with each word, image, or symbol meshing perfectly with all other words, images, and symbols, as in a series of well-lubricated cogs. This is so even if the forward thrust of the cogs is not made to eject, as it often is, the "message" the critic was predisposed to find. Evidence of blindness to defects or inconsistencies casts suspicion upon testimony about merits or consistencies. The most subtle and convincing verbal analysis of a fine passage loses authority when the critic finds identical virtues in a passage far from fine. The truth ceases to be true if it would be uttered whether it was true or not. What shall we think of praises of *Hamlet* by one who has raved over *Titus Andronicus?* For the idolater, all the works of the idol are equally or almost equally perfect.

Measure for Measure is a play with great merits and great defects. The defects are of kinds sometimes attributable to the author, sometimes to accidents of transmission, sometimes to either, we cannot tell which. They are often petty, like the discrepancy between "nineteen" and "fourteen," or between "Thomas Tapster" and "Pompey Bum." They are often less petty, like the rough structural joints (at several spots characters fall quite outside the class of the Capulet servant, by knowing a fact at one moment and proving ignorant of it the next), or like the incoherence of

> Then no more remaines
> But that, to your sufficiency, as your worth is able,
> And let them work:

and the thumping redundance of,

> Noueltie is onely in request, and as it is as dangerous to be aged in any kinde of course, as it is vertuous to be constant in any undertaking.

And, finally, they are in the aggregate the reverse of petty since they distort the entire conception. We seem to have, not one kind of play, but two, very imperfectly soldered together. We can even pinpoint the line where the fracture is so obvious that it cannot be ignored. After Claudio's "O hear me, Isabella" (III.i.151) all the major characters lose their capacity for emotional response, and can hear of black treachery, their own impending deaths, or the supposed death of loved ones with relative aplomb. Intrigue takes over, and Duke Vincentio ceases to resemble Harun-al-Rashid so much as he resembles Brainworm. There have been earlier signs that the playwright was heading for trouble.

The fact that the play contains some of the greatest scenes in Shakespeare, and some of the most marvelous poetry, does not alter the fact that it is not a success in the same sense in which *King Lear* is a success, or even *The Comedy of Errors* is a success. Of course we value it more than the latter, but we do so because of its parts. It had not, when it assumed its present form, crystallized into a satisfying artistic whole; and it is doubtful, in view of its materials, if it could ever have done so. The romantic and postromantic invectives against Isabella have been properly reproved by such historical critics as W. W. Lawrence and R. W. Chambers, but these knew when to stop in their work of rehabilitation. The merits and defects of the piece have been capably outlined by E. M. W. Tillyard[12] in the kind of essay usually patronized for its "common sense" (because it is uncommonly sensible), but the voice of moderation is not the voice which prevails.

The prevailing voices in Shakespearean criticism demonstrate pretty clearly that Lascelles Abercrombie's plea for "liberty of interpreting" has been followed by liberty of prophesying, and that the question we must now ask is not "How many children had Lady Macbeth?" but "How much sanctity had Duke Vincentio?" The impulse of the anti-Stratfordians to deify Shakespeare is being matched by the critical impulse to treat his works as holy writ. The commentary, whether it is accretive and rabbinical in character, or "analytical" and scholastic, or apocalyptic and inspired, is uniformly solemn. One would not guess that there are *laughs* in the play (or anywhere else in Shakespeare)—Pompey and Lucio, if they are mentioned at all, are always strangely etherealized. When such criticism is written from the viewpoint of the orthodox Catholic or Protestant, or the spokesman for Christian Humanism, it is relatively unembarrassing because there is at least an external point of reference and we can accept or reject the argument. But usually there is no stated body of belief to which we can refer. Shakespeare is Allah, and the Critic is his prophet. The only point of reference is the various notions which simmer about in the critic's mind. Not only does each detail in the play prove to articulate with all other details, but the whole expresses an "idea," unmistakable and yet hitherto mistaken, perfectly expressed, yet in need of "interpretation." Duke Vincentio emerges as a Christ figure, but a very peculiar Christ figure, and one sometimes sharing his ministry with Lucio—not the Lucio we thought we knew, but one prefiguring the divine spirit later made incarnate in D. H. Lawrence.

The interpretations of *Measure for Measure* offer only an extreme example. The other plays, especially the tragedies and romances, are receiving the same treatment. This kind of writing is less criticism than a misty form of apologetics, with its religiosity unrelated to any religion except incidentally—as in the re-establishment of a hell, whither Shakespeare's tragic heroes may be sent along with any critic who has (sentimentally) ever put in a good word for them. My intention, I repeat, is not to attack *Measure for Measure* or to imply that it is unworthy of thoughtful discussion. It is one of my favorite plays. My fear is that the idolatrous transformation of it into something it is *not* will rob us of the wonderful thing which, in parts, it really *is*. And that is the danger in general—that we shall trade our birthright of great artistry for a mess of third-rate philosophy.

I have refrained from mentioning particular names less

because it would be ungracious than because it would be unjust. The names which come to mind are not those of the uniquely idolatrous, but those of the most successfully so. I once heard a lecture by a former Paulist father who had become a Unitarian minister. It was called "From the Apostles to the Creeds." All that I now remember of it is that the speaker approved of the apostles but disapproved of the creeds—that, and the fact that he placed the time interval between the two at four hundred years. Perhaps the second circumstance is what made me recall the lecture in the year of Shakespeare's fourth centenary. And perhaps what I am really saying is that I am devoted to primitive Shakespeareanity. None of us can claim total immunity from the effects of the myth of perfection.

And yet we should combat it, in others and ourselves. It may well be that Shakespeare idolatry is drawing strength from something other than its roots in the past. Having lost their anchorage in the faith of their fathers, many are seeking a substitute in secular literature, and perhaps, in a materialistic age, any form of idealism has something to be said for it. But for some forms very little can be said—specifically, any that cannot be judged on their own merits, and cannot stand on their own feet, rather than on Shakespeare's. Besides, faith should begin where we reach the limits of knowledge.

We must still take into account who Shakespeare actually was and what he actually wrote. There remains a mission for the sons of Martha—the biographer studying documents rather than cryptograms, the textual student, the literary historian, even the rational critic. These have no large congregation—only a small audience—but I believe that they love Shakespeare and do honor his memory, this side idolatry, as much as any.

3 THESE OUR ACTORS

*I*N APRIL 1864 Shakespeare's birth was celebrated at Stratford in the fashion set nearly a century before at the
Garrick Jubilee, with bell-ringing, banquet, fireworks, fancy-
dress ball, and panegyrics in prose and verse. A balloon ascen-
sion was announced, but it had to be canceled owing to a
shortage of gas. Let us prudently refrain from comment—
qui mocat mocabitur. Since this was the tricentenary, the
feasting extended to London, where Charles Dickens joined
with some hardy dissidents in proposing a new way of paying
homage. The nation, said he, should establish a good school
for the children of actors, in part payment of its debt to
Shakespeare's "peculiar and precarious vocation" where each
striver "must earn every loaf of his bread in his own person,
with the aid of his own face, his own limbs, his own voice,
his own memory, and his own life and spirits, and these
failing, he fails."[1] Dickens was saying that acting is a heroic
profession, a lifetime of balancing on the high wire without
the safety net of tenure, sick leave, or company pensions.
With characteristic freedom from humbug, he was not
implying that it is a priesthood of art, its members all radiant
with sacred Shakespearean fire.

One would not wish to alter his terms, but it may be
pointed out that, in 1864, a bow to the acting profession
was appropriate at a Shakespeare celebration. From the time
of Burbage in the early seventeenth century until that of
Irving in the late nineteenth, every leading English and
American actor was a Shakespearean actor. During the three
centuries in which actors controlled the English-speaking
stage, the plays of Shakespeare dominated the repertory.
We need not assume that this was a good thing—in some of

its practical effects it was the reverse—but it does establish a unique bond between a particular craftsman and later followers of his craft. Certainly it renders obligatory, in even the briefest survey of conceptions of Shakespeare, a look at the stance of those whom he himself called "the abstract and brief chronicles of the time."

We are confronted at once with a paradox. The actors as actors have served Shakespeare well through the ages, perhaps better than the biographers and critics, but these same actors as wardens of the Shakespearean theatrical enterprise have served him far from well. Some of the most perceptive of our ancestors in each generation have admired the leading Shakespearean actors at the same time that they have despised their productions. The constant disparity in merit between the performance of the great parts and the performance of plays as wholes must have an explanation. I shall try to explain it in terms of the *afterimage*. The actor is by the very nature of his calling a *popular* man. He must be so or perish. It is perhaps inevitable that he should see Shakespeare as a perennially *popular* dramatist or not see him at all.

It is a pleasure to begin with the credit side of the balance sheet. I have not sojourned among the old actors with the rewarding love of scholars like Odell and Sprague, but I have done some friendly visiting. The common generalizations about them are all libels—for instance that they are inordinately vain, or that they are profligate as a class, or that they are empty-minded folk "reverberating hollowness." No profession comparably small has left so many interesting letters, diaries, and other memorabilia, or produced a larger number of articulate and active-minded notables. We are no longer bewitched by their masks but we can still relish the mind of a Garrick, a Macready, a Fanny Kemble, or an Edwin Booth. The safest generalization about the actors as people is that those who have risen to the top of the profession have tended to be superior people.

The most surprising thing about the leaders is that generalization proves difficult even in the matter of their apparent elementary qualifications. Considering that nearly all played with distinction parts as various as those of Romeo and Lear, Shylock and Brutus, Hamlet and Othello, Macbeth and Benedick, we might assume that each possessed the kind of mimetic versatility conferred by a perfect physique. Such proves far from the case. Among the famous early Hamlets, for instance, the most uniform physical characteristic seems to have been corpulence, Betterton inheriting from his predecessors both an interpretation of the role and an ample girth, so that we can less easily visualize him as the sad lover and taut young Prince than as the aging justice "in fair round belly with good capon lined." In addition Betterton is said to have been handicapped with a "low and grumbling" voice,[2] although this is hard to believe since, traditionally, a good voice had been the ticket of entrance to the acting profession. Garrick was conspicuously short, five feet four inches. Kean also was below average height. Macready had a flat and homely face. Many considered Irving as poorly coordinated, in fact awkward. Judging by their portraits, only the elder Kemble and the younger Booth seem really to belong in the royal succession. Although the others were well endowed in some of the external attributes—of person, limbs, face, voice, mentioned by Dickens—none could have won a contest in his times, or even in his own company, if the criterion were perfection of face and form.

The strength of the leaders was internal. All had immense stamina, permitting them to play exhausting roles night after night, season after season, in spite of a crushing burden of duties in theatrical management and in what would now be called public relations. Their ability to achieve concert pitch, to come fully alive and "project" at the moment the curtain rose, was independent of youth, health, prosperity, or even encouragement. Hundreds have testified to their magnetism—to the fact that the moment they appeared one simply had to look at them, the "well-graced" in contrast to "him that enters next." [3] The quality explains something, but not enough. All public men have energizing force, high voltage, and the fact that a Garrick had it explains why he was a leader but not why he was a great actor. Actors could have it without being great, Edwin Forrest for instance, who would have been a leader in any kind of public activity and might have done better as a congressman.

The indispensable gift of the fine actor seems to be a peculiar kind of imagination, at once sympathetic and detached, coupled with a craftsman's concern with technique. He must understand human character by instinct, and communicate his understanding by inspired trickery. Shakespeare's unique gift for responding to life as Everyman found its perfect use in his work as an actor writing for actors. His ability to get inside of his fictive persons, to see, think, love, hate, hope, and despair with them, may be thought of as a high form of mimicry. But if his imagination was sympathetic, so also was it detached—or at least detachable. He could get out of his persons as well as into them, which is to say that he never became his characters and they never became merely him—not his mouthpieces and stand-ins, but discriminable *identities* abiding his and our judgment. Shakespeare as poet composed lines which Shakespeare as actor would be happy to speak in creating illusions of reality, and although he knew as he wrote that most of the lines would be spoken by actors other than himself, he was so closely integrated with his troupe that his interest in all the lines was proprietary. Granville-Barker once said that he supplied "raw materials" for actors,[4] and although the phrase is unhappily chosen, we can accept it in the sense that he provided actors with maximum opportunity. The good ones have perpetually rediscovered this. The Baconians and their successors have won no converts among actors, not because of the latter's *amour propre,* but because they detect in the plays the presence of a colleague, one might almost say a fellow conspirator. Those who dismiss Shakespeare as a "mere actor" must be unaware that Sophocles and Molière, the only other dramatists always listed with the literary immortals, were also actors in the plays they wrote.

I have proposed the gift of an imagination at once sympathetic and detached as the great essential, not on theoretical ground but on that of historical evidence: the finest actors all had it. The word of highest praise bestowed on the leader in each age was always the same—the word "natural" or its early equivalent, "true." After Burbage, who played so "truly," Betterton, then Garrick, then each heir in the royal succession was praised as greatest because he was so "natural." Each succeeded to his crown after a brief interregnum in which no single actor was sufficiently "natural" to win universal praise.

Now as we survey the theatrical illustration of the past, even the portraits of the leading actors in their roles as executed by leading painters, we are struck by an artificiality almost ludicrous. Obviously the word "natural" did not mean realistic or restrained. We arrive at the meaning when we recall that "natural" was the word of supreme praise always bestowed on Shakespeare's plays themselves. It meant, not that they presented life realistically or in the language of ordinary speech, but that they told truths about men and women; in this sense only were they "nature itself." As applied to the leading actors, it meant, not that they spoke in conversational tones or conducted themselves like one's friends in the coffeehouse—of course they did not—but that their acting carried conviction: they seemed to understand and believe what they were saying, and to feel the emotions they were simulating. The tones and gestures might be highly conventional, meaning those currently negotiable as symbols of ideas and emotions, and quite different tones and gestures might prove viable in different ages—the style could change, and the actor must master, adapt, or create a style, but his "naturalness" did not reside ultimately in the style. The style of John Kemble was stately, that of Edmund Kean the reverse, but this means only that neoclassic ideals had yielded to romantic ideals, not *unnaturalness* to *naturalness*. Kemble seemed natural enough to an observer as perceptive as Sir Walter Scott,[5] and Kemble's sister, Mrs. Siddons, as Lady Macbeth seemed to everyone to be "nature itself."

Acting cannot be judged by what it appears in itself to be, but only by what it appears to effect. To modern theatergoers the acting styles of the nineteenth-, eighteenth-, and seventeenth-century stars would probably seem equally formalized and overemphatic, but we would be mistaken in thinking that present-day styles are truly realistic. The actor who stands, or more frequently lies prone, baring his heart in a languid mutter, is not behaving as do actual people, who are still tense, emphatic, and voluble when emotionally perturbed, but is expressing in a highly conventional way what people are now supposed to feel, "the hopelessness of it all." We see few actual people conducting themselves in this way, and those who do are usually imitating the actors, as life imitates art.

Let us look for a moment at the Shakespearean tradition in reference to this single point—of artificial overemphasis. That the actor should accompany speech with illustrative gesture, should "suit the action to the word," was assumed, and of course the assumption could lead to mechanical compliance. In the less gifted actor it is the mechanical compliance which one observes. Even in my own youth, early in this century, it might have been said that the only person who felt obliged to nod vigorously each time he said yes was a small child, a country bumpkin, or a Shakespearean actor. But the masters of the past have always known that the ideal underlying the tradition was to explicate lines and express emotion, not to repeat meanings and step upon metaphors; hence these masters have never looked upward whenever they mentioned the stars or flapped their arms as they spoke of the flight of crows to "the rooky wood." Although the approved and adopted method of expressing an emotion, such as the frenzied clutch at one's hair, might be in fact extreme, its currency was such that it would function as a thing of custom, almost like the player's garment, leaving the gifted performer still free to be "natural." He cunningly modified the inherited postures, or slipped his interpretation into the interstices.

Traditionally the ghost of Hamlet's father stood quite still, evidently on the principle that the dead are immobilized, but a start of fright by Hamlet upon first seeing the ghost was obligatory. Actors competed in this start of fright, and we have Johnson's barbed comment that Garrick's was such as might frighten the Ghost. We cannot build upon this detail our idea of Garrick's style, and certainly not of its effect. Another ghostly encounter proves that Garrick did not signal fright mechanically with galvanic starts. One of the few bits of "business" known to have descended from the time of Burbage was Macbeth's dropping of a wine goblet when he first sees Banquo's ghost. The Macbeths between Betterton and Garrick, in a deteriorated style, had been dashing the goblet to the floor. Garrick let it slip slowly from his nerveless hand. Garrick as Lear, awakening in the arms of Cordelia and saying "Are these tears wet?" touched his daughter's cheek and looked at his finger. Thus described, the gesture seems simply banal, as if proof were being offered that tears are indubitably wet, but the effect of the gesture as Garrick employed it was to reveal the speaker's incredulous wonder as he emerges from his stupor. Although we need no assurance that tears are wet, this man does, just as he needs assurance that his daughter is real. Far from being either banal or extreme, the effect, in the observer's word, was "exquisite." [6]

In trying to evaluate a "style" we are always in error if we cut in at a particular point and miss sight of the sustaining tradition which it both modifies and preserves. The great actors retained the best of what their predecessors had done, and made the best innovations—*best* in the sense of being both striking and "natural." The inferior actors were the apes of the great ones or else the inventors of gestures and business which failed to convince. The word for these was "wrong"—the theatrical antonym for "natural." Those who acted wholly outside the tradition, the visiting foreign luminaries such as Salvini, Fechter, and Bernhardt, proved initially exciting, but the final verdict upon them was negative. The reason is clear. Fechter, in playing Othello about to slay Desdemona, illustrated the line "It is the cause, the cause, my soul!" by gazing into a mirror, then casting it away with a grimace of disgust, thus pointing to the blackness of his skin as the simple cause of the catastrophe. It is a clever idea, like the clever ideas now inundating the modern director's theater, but it is "wrong" and its "wrongness" was perceived by the discriminating. Dickens wrote a favorable advance notice of Fechter at the time of his American tour—praising, for instance, the straight flaxen hair of his Hamlet as compared with the traditional curly black wig—but Dickens was attacking the small "prescriptions" followed mechanically by minor actors, and he enjoyed Fechter's "piratical swoop" upon these.[7] More durable satisfaction was supplied by an Edwin Booth, who accepted or rejected the business of his father, of Edmund Kean, and of other predecessors only after long and patient study.

I have yet to define what it was about the acting of the leaders which struck their contemporaries as so "natural" in spite of accompanying styles which would seem to us both formalized and overemphatic. Let me quote first a fragment of commentary by Leigh Hunt, which suggests a fusion of the highly exaggerated with the "true to life." It was agreed that Charles Kemble was not the master his brother had been, but, in speaking of his Benedick, Hunt gives credit where credit is due:

His utterance of his grand final reason for marrying—"The world must be peopled"—with his hands linked behind him, a general elevation of his aspect, and a sort of look at the whole universe before him, as if he saw all the future generations that might depend on his verdict, was a bit of the right masterly gusto—the true perception and relish of the thing.[8]

Mark the words—*the true perception and relish of the thing* —a perfect identification, not of the "realistic," but of the "natural," in its proper theatrical magnification.

In the earliest extant refined description of an actor in the role of Hamlet, Cibber tells how Betterton played the Prince's first encounter with his father's ghost. The "passion," said Cibber, was "an almost breathless astonishment, or an impatience, limited by filial reverence . . ."

This was the light into which Betterton threw this scene, which he open'd with a pause of mute amazement: then rising slowly to a solemn, trembling voice, he made the ghost equally terrible to the spectator as to himself, and in the descriptive part of the natural emotions which the ghastly vision gave him, the boldness of his expostulations was still govern'd by decency, manly but not braving; his voice never rising into that seeming outrage or wild defiance of what he naturally rever'd.[9]

The justness of Betterton's interpretation need not concern us here. The relevant fact is that Cibber had been impressed not with the mere temperance in the whirlwind of passion "that may give it smoothness," but with the fact that several levels of feeling had been simultaneously communicated—the excitement and terror, yet tenderness and respect—reflecting the complexity of *nature*.

The success of the great actors in conveying precisely this impression has left countless testimonials. I shall cite only one more. Here are glimpses of Macready's Lear as provided by the fine observer Charles Dickens. In the first scene,

something beyond the turbulent greatness or royal impotence of Lear had been presented—something to redeeem him from his treatment of Cordelia. The bewildered pause after giving his "father's heart" away—the hurry yet hesitation of his manner as he orders France to be called—"Who stirs? Call Burgundy"—has told us at once how much consideration he needed, how much pity . . .

And in the fourth scene, after the line "Since my young lady's going into France, sir, the Fool hath much pined away"—

Mr. Macready's manner of turning off at this with an expression of half impatience, half ill-repressed emotion—"No more of that, I have noted it well"—was inexpressibly touching. We saw him in the secret corner of his heart, still clinging to the memory of her who was used to be his best object . . . "most best, most dearest." [10]

Now despite the difference in data provided by a Hamlet and a Lear, and despite the gulf in time and temperament separating a Betterton and Cibber from a Macready and Dickens, we observe the persistence of an ideal. Acting was great, was *natural,* when it was not reductive—when it escaped the hazard of flattening characters into silhouettes. By what means, what tones and gestures, the Bettertons, Garricks, and Macreadys created illusions of inwardness matters not in the least. They succeeded in creating them.

Macready's "hurry yet hesitation," his "half impatience, half ill-repressed emotion," like Betterton's more grandiloquently described "passion . . . limited by filial reverence"— in general, the half-this, half-that of the actor—compares well with the all-this, or all-that reductions often proffered by the oversimplifying or overreaching critic. Sometimes the critic seems positively hostile to the character he analyzes, as he tries to rip out the heart of the mystery and succeeds only in fortifying our distaste for evisceration. In contrast, the gifted actor synthesizes and fulfills. The oft-quoted early pronouncement that the good player is the "best commentator," [11] is true, not in respect to his offstage generalizations, which are often commonplace and sometimes puerile, but in respect to his ability to display an instinctive understanding of particular roles. The great ones could get inside of Hamlet, Lear, Macbeth, Othello, and still feel at home in Shylock. Shakespeare had limited his demands. He had not required his players to inhabit the bodies of monsters. On those few occasions when he created the monstrous, a Richard Bunchback, Goneril, or Caliban, he had supplied at least some human accommodations, a few familiar grips and footholds. The great performers seem to have had a kind of heart knowledge even of the direst villains. Mrs. Siddons' portrayal of Lady Macbeth was terrifying, yet "natural," and its sympathetic element must not have been unrelated to the fact that Mrs. Siddons had some quite tolerant things to say offstage about this maimed spirit. The great actors never portrayed Hamlet as anything but admirable, the noble, aspiring, cruelly afflicted Prince, never the weak, and even sinister, figure often encountered in criticism. His incestuous drives evaded the insight of actors until they supplemented their reading of the play by the reading of a Freudian critique. Only one critical word about *King Lear* has descended to us from Shakespeare's own age. It describes Burbage's playing of the ancient king. The word is not "old" Lear, as one might expect, since Burbage is adjacently praised as "young" Hamlet—nor is it "mad" Lear, or "poor" Lear. The word is "kind" Lear,[12] suggesting that Burbage's interpretation was sympathetic—and right.

I have one more sprig for my garland of homage to the old actors, and will add it even though I must use a word no longer in good repute: the great ones were great *elocutionists*. They delivered brilliantly the celebrated passages—those orations, soliloquies, and dramatic lyrics which audiences had come to regard as familiar arias. Failure with these could cancel success with everything else, and they were studied anew with loving care and delivered as with a caress. How delightful it is to hear the superb speeches properly spoken all of us know who have listened to our few remaining adepts. Shakespeare's language was scored for the human voice, and to hear it rendered by the right voice is to hear the music rightly played. Cibber has told us how, in his address to the Ghost, Betterton "opened with a pause." All of his masterly successors were masters of the pause—and of disengagement from "business" as poetry was permitted to reign. If the Ghost of Hamlet's father was the only character who stood consistently still, Hamlet himself and the others, as played by the illustrious, stood still at enchanted and enchanting moments, their very immobility a gesture and the most effective of all. At such moments the actor's voice echoed in a well of silence, and these times of perfect rapport, of silence audible, were the actor's private guerdon even though applause was the currency with which he bought his bread. Walt Whitman remembered after fifty years the quiet

entrance of Junius Booth as Richard III and then, as Whitman says, "the perfect following hush of perhaps three
thousand people waiting"[13]—

> Now is the winter of our discontent
> Made glorious summer by this sun of York . . .

With so much granted the grand succession of leading
Shakespearean actors, can anything important be taken
away? I regret to say that it can, and I turn now to the debit
column. What Whitman heard was a fine rendition of
Shakespearean speeches, and what he saw was a fine characterization of Richard, but he neither heard nor saw Shakespeare's play. Booth, like all the others, played Cibber's
adaptation, and although it was the least injurious of the lot,
its very success lent encouragement to the manglers. Betterton was a great Hamlet, but he introduced into *A Midsummer Night's Dream* dances by six monkeys and twenty-
four Chinamen. Irving was disinclined to admit into his
acting versions non-Shakespearean writing, but he sometimes omitted more than half of what Shakespeare himself
had written and rearranged what was left. We may ignore
entirely the notorious adaptations, by Davenant, Dryden,
Settle, Tate, Cibber, Garrick, and the rest, and limit our view
to what purported to be Shakespeare's "true and original
texts restored." Our lamentable discovery is that no such
thing was used by the players from the time of Betterton to
the time of Irving, and that the meddling had begun even
before Burbage's death. At the very least there were inter-
polated shows and the cutting and rearranging of lines.

The redundant intrusion of scenic effects is a fact so
familiar that it need not be dwelled upon. Even before 1623
the Witches in *Macbeth* had conjured up for themselves
some non-Shakespearean cohorts to sing and dance, and by
1667 they had begun to fly on theatrical wires. Something

like Betterton's irrelevant monkeys and Chinamen invaded every production of every play, between the "acts" and in them. The invading elements did not have to be frivolous in order to destroy the balance of a play. For instance, *Romeo and Juliet* soon began to open with a pitched battle between rival power lords, strewing the stage with corpses, instead of with the clownish squabble and undignified melee with which Shakespeare had defined at once the stale stupidity of the Montague-Capulet feud. Since funeral processions "took," or as we might say "went over big," vast ones were introduced upon slight pretexts, including one for Juliet before she was really dead. The nineteenth century showed some improvement over the eighteenth in fidelity to Shakespeare's words, but not in other respects. Sheer massiveness of scenic effects smothered everything but the performance of the star. In the Roman plays more "senators" assembled on certain stages than could have been mustered in ancient Rome.

Even in productions where good taste or frugality imposed a relative spareness, the plays were mutilated by the "point" (a piece of arbitrary emphasis resembling a bird dog's flushing of a quail), the "picture" (the freezing of a stage group in an ornamental pose designed to win first a sigh of ecstasy and then a storm of applause), and the "strong curtain." The last is the best single illustration of the prevailing ignorance of and indifference to Shakespeare's own stage and dramatic art. Since the plays were originally designed for a curtainless stage, the typical scene tends to diminish in intensity toward its very end, so that the ensuing scene, necessarily beginning at less than highest pitch, may successfully blend in and have a chance of winning immediate attention. Putting it crudely, the scenes tend to fade out rather than black out, for the general good of the play. Shakespeare made an artistic virtue of theatrical necessity by letting his most compelling scenes end in quiet reverberations, choral in effect. Particular experience is absorbed into general experience as wider vistas return and we catch glimpses of the skyline. For instance, the horrifying scene in which Gloucester's eyes are put out does not end in horror, but with the hushed accents of pitying servants resolved to help an injured old man. The hilarious scene at the Cheapside tavern where Falstaff tells his lies about thieves in buckram and acts the part of king does not end in hilarity, but in Hal's sober remarks about returning stolen money and meeting the obligations of the morrow.

But on the picture-frame stages the curtain was there—and the chance to end every scene with a bang. Along with "minor" characters and "minor" dialogues, the scene endings in "minor" key had to go. The result was a change in the mood, texture, the very direction of the plays. The trial scene in *The Merchant of Venice* must end with Shylock's exit in defeat, its relaxed aftermath lopped off. In fact the whole performance sometimes ended in this exit, with the whole fifth act lopped off—that wonderful part for which the rest was made! It is amazing that even after the portrayal of Shylock had been sentimentalized, the "strong curtain" was provided, so that the play ceased to tell of the triumph of love over hate, but rather of the triumph of Christians over a Jew. And yet the part of the Jew himself might be excellently acted. Audiences saw Shylock but not *The Merchant of Venice*.

Hamlet usually ended when the actor playing the Prince had no more lines to speak. The entrance of Fortinbras was deleted. The age which coined the phrase "*Hamlet* without the Prince" staged the Prince without the play, just as the age preceding had played tragic *Lear* without the tragedy. It is little wonder that the very men who so admired the great Shakespearean actors so despised the theater they perpetuated.

Much ignorant obloquy has fallen upon Charles Lamb for attacking the Shakespearean theater when his only guilt was to say well what most intelligent men thought. At one time or other Johnson, Morgann, Goethe, Hazlitt, Coleridge, and the rest who head the roster of perceptive commentators said substantially the same thing. Their fine insights derived necessarily from their reading, because the plays as they were written were otherwise unavailable. When Coleridge said that hearing Edmund Kean was "like reading Shakespeare by flashes of lightning," he was well aware of the encompassing darkness, indeed was inclined to believe that productions should be forbidden by law. Shelley and Keats, for all their youthful enthusiasm, love of Shakespeare, and star-struck respect for Kean, had no illusions about the merit of the productions.

If there were good actors and bad productions for centuries, in ages as various as the Restoration, the Augustan, the Johnsonian, the Romantic, and the Victorian, there must be a reason why. If we try to explain it in terms of external theatrical history—of stage structure, auditorium capacity and acoustics, the licensing act, monopoly, and the like—we are describing symptoms and not diagnosing the malady. The true explanation, I believe, is that Shakespeare was not really what the leaders in the theatrical profession imagined him to be. We can say that he was the greatest dramatist of all times with our eyes open—the image is true. But we can say he was the greatest dramatist *for* all times only with our eyes closed—the image is false. To take Jonson's "not of an age but for all times" in a literal sense, and try to give it practical application, is to break our shins on a metaphor. Art may be "universal" without being universally appealing, and when we use such a word of praise, we are speaking metaphorically about the approbation which certain works deserve, not that which, on statistical evidence, they receive; otherwise the Metropolitan Museum of Art would be more crowded than the Grand Central Station, and the New York Symphony concerts would have to be held in Madison Square Garden. True, the theater in its origins and traditions is a *popular* institution, and Shakespeare wrote the most *popular* Elizabethan plays, but it does not follow that he wrote the most popular Restoration, Augustan, Romantic, and Victorian plays. By assuming that he had done so, the managing actors forced the plays into a false mold, maiming them in the process. If they were not still the most popular plays, they could be made so. Shakespeare the popular artist became Shakespeare the popularized artist. The popular is often great. The popularized is always small.

One encounters not infrequently a tacit sentiment for leaving certain truths unspoken, either because they savor of snobbish "exclusiveness" or because they are less useful than pious fictions. This is not the occasion to debate the matter. The fact remains that as early as 1660 the playwright of the relatively many had become the playwright of the relatively few. Shakespeare had already become a writer of primary interest only to the literary. As the total number of enthusiastic readers constantly increased, the proportion of receptive theatergoers constantly decreased, however the fact may have been disguised by traffic in falsely labeled substitutes. The situation was as inevitable as the succession of generations. Only the few in any age truly savor the art of the past. We need only look about us, at our most intelligent and cultivated friends—uniformly inoculated with the "classics" in college and immune to them ever after—to recognize that this is so. The living are alert to the contemporary voice, to the artistic statements of their own time, poor things perhaps but their own. The actors played Shakespeare because they knew he was great, but they played him as they did because they were trying to preserve his popularity. In consequence their service neither to Shakespeare nor to the people was of a high order.

The primary duty of those who control theaters is to the drama of their own era. The pseudo-Shakespearean dominance of the repertory proved something of an incubus. It helps to explain why the only post-Elizabethan drama upon which we place value was written in the brief periods escaping that dominance. In the eighteenth century, the potentially fine playwright Oliver Goldsmith complained that he was flogged into silence by "Will" and to a lesser extent by "Ben." The romantic period, with its ready poets and rich dramatic potential, created, as original plays, only attentuated Shakespeare. Critics like Archer and Shaw were, of course, right when they fought the battle of Ibsen and the moderns, even though they misrepresented the opposition.

The productions of the famous succession of actor-managers from Betterton to Irving were designed not for a moderate-sized voluntary public but for a large involuntary one—involuntary in the sense that it would not take Shakespeare straight. It could enjoy some of the poetry of the playwright, but not the plays as poetry. It could take interest in a great character like Hamlet, Othello, or Macbeth, but not in that character's universe. It could be seduced by gratuitous shows and scenic splendors, and pricked into response by the "point," the "picture," the "strong curtain," and similar claptrap. An equivalent to the productions was the vast amount of Shakespeareana designed for popular sale—the collections of "memory gems" and picture books, and the disquisitions upon the "characters." The best of these were good, like the interpretations of the good actors, but on the average they were poor. Often they bore only a coincidental relationship to Shakespeare's plays, although they might teach useful lessons, provide touching tributes to womanhood, or reach into the dark backward and abysm of time to describe the girlhood of Shakespeare's heroines. Still there were more good critical works for intelligent men to read than good productions for them to see. In every audience there would have been a cheated minority—those who shared the interest in heroes and love of rhetoric displayed by the average spectator, but who were also capable of accepting a play as a unified work of art. These were offered instead an overillustrated collection of memory gems and characters.

I began with an offering to the memory of the great Shakespearean actors. I then proceeded to take away. At the moment I am left with the sensation of having taken too much, and I should like in conclusion to strike a balance. Since the fabric of our Shakespearean heritage must remain intact so long as true texts are printed, we cannot accuse the actors of destroying the materials they used. The case against their theater rests less upon what it did than upon what it failed to do—provide occasional performances of Shakespeare's plays for those who really wanted to see them. This neglected band would have included not just the circle of Lamb and Keats, but a quite considerable number, had they ever been given a chance to get together. Their counterparts across the Channel were able to see the plays of Molière and Racine as written, and we are unwilling to concede that such privilege is purchasable only at the price of political tyranny. No doubt the productions designed to woo the many were better than nothing and, aside from their effect in restaint of free theatrical trade, did more good than harm. Certainly they served "culture" better than the accidentally-but-aptly named "illegitimate" drama.

I began by dwelling upon the true talent and effectiveness of the great performers. Let me add a tribute to their purity of motive. They popularized Shakespeare because of their conviction that he deserved to be popular. They wished to speak his lines because of their conviction that none better had ever been written. They risked bankruptcy in their expenditures upon processions, scenes, and senators, not alone as a bid for patronage but because they thought Shakespeare should not be done cheap. And finally, although they perverted his art, they did not pervert his morality.

As a boy I had a glimpse into their world. It was too late to see Edwin Booth and the visiting English stars he had rivaled, but not too late to see Shakespeare on Philadelphia stages where Booth and these rivals had performed. The atmosphere, the staging, the lighting, possibly some of the scenery, and certainly some of the dust came straight out of the nineteenth century. There I saw in their latter days Sothern and Marlowe, Robert Mantell, and similar tail-enders in the ancient procession. I recall that I was deeply impressed by Robert Mantell in scarlet robes as he threatened to hurl the "cur-r-r-se of R-r-rome" upon the head of anyone who dared step within a holy circle which he drew with a magnificent gesture about a certain pure and white-clad maiden. My father responded to my praise of Shakespeare by telling me gently that this piece happened to be by a different fellow. I was taken also to the theaters of the neighborhood stock companies, where virtue and vice were locked in an eternal death grip, and where one could always count on a good storm—paper snow falling upon hapless orphans, icy wind blowing horizontal the rags of elderly couples driven from their foreclosed homes, and similar delights. When I was old enough to go alone, my parents showed some concern about the billing: *Dr. Jekyll and Mr. Hyde* was barely permissible, and *St. Elmo* not at all, but anything by Shakespeare performed by anyone anywhere was all right—Shakespeare was noble and good. A lifetime of study has failed to reveal to me any serious flaw in their impression, and it had been conveyed to them by the old actors. Whatever they did to his artistry, they held aloft his moral torch with a zeal almost hierophantic.

In England the actors did not get the school for their children advocated by Dickens, but the last leaders got knighthood from Queen Victoria. They deserved it. The "regulars" who went to Irving's Lyceum and to Benson's Theatre Royal at Stratford have left testimonials to them as places of innocence and joy. These our actors—Burbage, Betterton, Garrick, Kemble, Kean, and the rest—have all melted into air, into thin air. Burbage was the first and last to give the audience Shakespeare, but the others gave a decent token. The twentieth century has demonstrated that the Shakespearean theater can give us somehing better—and also something worse.

*P*LAYGOING is a seductive topic, like old songs, tempting one to nostalgic reminiscence, but theatrical souvenirs, however dear to oneself, are as boring to others as the rehearsal of dreams. I shall not linger long with mine. I have told how my earliest experience of Shakespeare in the theater offered a glimpse of the old tradition of the actor-managers, as I saw Sothern and Mantell playing, in their late autumn, in the old theaters in the old manner. In the period immediately following I saw such actors as Fritz Lieber, John Barrymore, and Walter Hampden in slightly more sophisticated but essentially the same kind of productions—with "strong curtains," long waits while the scenery was being shifted about, and minor roles diminished to flickers by the luminosity of the "star."

Then in the late twenties came something so different as to seem like a revelation—the productions of the Stratford Memorial Company on tour under the direction of Bridges-Adams. We left the performances with the sensation that we had never seen Shakespeare staged before. In place of overstuffed museum pieces, suffered through as a cultural rite, were actual plays, lovely and alive. Among my grateful acquaintances, groping for analogies, the remark most often made was "It was like the Symphony"—the supreme accolade since the Philadelphia Orchestra was our proudest local possession. The speakers had heard Beethoven properly played. They had never before heard Shakespeare played with comparable fidelity, not to mention comparable intelligence and integrated skills. The productions had genuine grace—they were honest and simple and moving.

It is significant that, in referring to this company, one mentions the director instead of the leading actors, although the latter were excellent and well known. For Shakespearean productions, as for all others, the actors' theater of former centuries had become the directors' theater of our own. At the same time, Shakespearean productions had become "revivals" —that is, sporadic instead of continuous in centrally located theaters. Shakespeare in repertory had disappeared in America, and had retreated in England to Stratford, Birmingham, Norwich, and the Old Vic. From these bastions it has since sallied forth to establish itself in Stratford, Connecticut, in Stratford, Ontario, and in a score of "festival" centers in the old country and the new. The Shakespearean stage has been institutionalized and, in a measure, subsidized. One may feel nostalgia for the old days when it was a natural survival fostered by the followers of Shakespeare's "peculiar and precarious" vocation, but the change was bound to come. Our hope is that it has not come too late.

Just a word on how the change came about. At the same time that Irving and then Tree were topping the tradition of scenic productions of "arranged" texts, William Poel was valiantly staging Shakespeare in what he believed to be the "Elizabethan manner." He had been anticipated, at least in regard to the paring away of excess scenic fat, by Continental producers, and even by Phelps and Benson, but no one hitherto had come forth as the declared propagandist and revolutionary. The direction of his experiments were best intimated to Americans by the Ben Greet players on tours which provoked more curiosity than enthusiasm. Poel's productions were technically inept, and blighted by an antiquarianism which is death to dramatic illusion, but he paved the way for men more talented than himself—Granville-Barker and Bridges-Adams, both originally associated with him. These abstracted from his experiments, and from their own knowledge and good taste, the best of the "Elizabethan" qualities—respect for the original script, nearly continuous performance upon a platform simply set, and a concern for troupe proficiency as distinct from the glamorous potential of the star. No capital was made of the mere novelty of the method, and the emphasis was placed upon the play as a unified artistic whole.

These men were lovers of poetry as well as the theater, and both were thoroughly knowledgeable. Granville-Barker has left us some of the best Shakespearean criticism of our century, and would have been capable of writing, as Bridges-Adams ultimately did write, a history of the Elizabethan stage.[1] In view of their unique qualifications, as scholars with literary taste and as professional men of the theater, what I say of their productions should not seem extravagant. They were probably the best that had been seen anywhere since the time of Shakespeare himself. Such a statement is always justly suspect, but lest I seem to be clinging to the illusions of my youth, I must point out that if such were the case my heroes should be Sothern, Mantell, Barrymore, and Hampden. As a matter of fact there were many critics in the twenties who had so fallen in love with the accretions of the traditional manner that they condemned the simplified productions as "un-Shakespearean." These were apt to say (upon authority somewhat obscure) that Shakespeare would have *loved* rich scenery, including the practicable forests, the wing-to-wing carpeting of turf, and even the live rabbits which hopped about in Arden. Presumably, he would also have *loved* the hacking of his poem to bits.

Granville-Barker and Bridges-Adams never received adequate support, but the excellence and integrity of their work did more than anything else to demonstrate that Shakespearean production needs and deserves financial subvention. This is no place for a review of theatrical economic history, even were I capable of offering one, but it is common knowl-

edge that at the turn of the century the Shakespearean theater
was dead as a solvent enterprise. By means of the popularizing techniques I have formerly described, and by practicing
brinkmanship with bankruptcy, the actor-managers had kept
the enterprise going, but their efforts, however heroic, had
succeeded only in obscuring the issues. Classical music, art,
and literature had been supported in publicly and privately
endowed academies, museums, and libraries for generations
before it seems to have occurred to anyone that classical
English drama might be worthy of similar support. Such
little support as there was had been limited to the theater
at Stratford as a local memorial under the patronage of the
Flowers.

A significant event occurred in 1914 when a philanthropist
contributed £25,000 to a "Home for Shakespeare" at the Old
Vic. The gesture could not have been wholly unrelated to
what Granville-Barker had been doing since 1912 at the
Savoy. In the wake of the Bridges-Adams tours of America
came the bulk of the funds from subscription which built
the present Stratford theater. The two Stratford theaters on
this side of the Atlantic have been built and in part maintained by public and private contributions, including grants
from the foundations. England now has a new National
Theatre made possible by the allocation of public funds, and
we may one day have such a theater ourselves. Then there
are the newly rising civic theaters. Even when Shakespearean
productions are not their avowed *raison d'être,* the figure of
the bard hovers promisingly in the wings. Shakespeare, in
addition to his other accomplishments, has proved an effective money-raiser. Nearly all of the summer "festivals"
operated in his honor receive financial assistance from colleges
and communities.

It is no longer assumed that public offerings of the works
of Shakespeare, unlike public offerings of the works of the

master painters and musicians, ought to "pay for themselves," and in this fact we should rejoice. However, there are factors to temper our joy. No one who faithfully samples the Shakespearean fare made available in the new facilities can believe that our problems are all solved. He may even wonder, after some especially harrowing experience, whether we have entered into a period of inflation and created a Shakespeare "bubble"—with the availability of performances in excess of true demand. A "festival" is established with financial assistance, but the maintenance of a performing company remains largely the responsibility of the box office. Seats must be sold to near capacity if the festival is to survive—and be eligible for further subvention. If a voluntary audience of sufficient size proves unavailable, an involuntary one must be enticed, and we are right back in the bad old days of popularization. The popularizing techniques of the twentieth century are different from those of the past, but not necessarily superior.

Let me return to my refrain of the afterimage. The actor-managers, as I have pointed out, saw Shakespeare as the perennially popular dramatist and strove to make him conform to the image. However, they were compelled by their professional bias to see him also as the creator of "parts"— Hamlet's, Othello's, Shylock's, and so on—and their imaginative affinity was with these "parts" rather than with the creator of them. They were inhibited from seeing themselves as author, and hence from gratuitously substituting ideas of their own for the ideas of the plays. Experience has taught us that the average twentieth-century director is not so inhibited. Himself neither an author nor an actor, and yet naturally inclined to see his function as creative, he tends to identify with the author. He sees Shakespeare as himself, or as his alter ego and collaborator. As living member of the team, the director is in a position of peculiar power and peculiar temptation.

Perhaps abuses are inherent in the directorial system itself, so that it is too much to expect anyone but titans to avoid them, and titans are rare in all callings. The very term "director" is ominous, suggesting one who issues "directives" and propels rather than leads. It is only slightly preferable to "producer"—which suggests the production of rabbits from hats. One wishes that the term "conductor" had been assimilated into the language of the theater and had proved as appropriate there as in the halls of the symphony. The director, having no play to create like the author, and no role to create like the actor, feels that he must create *direction,* and becomes a middleman or processer. Sometimes he becomes a kind of Nick Bottom, the author and actor manqué, playing all the parts extempore. Too often he adopts the modern view that knowledge is hostile to creativity, and proudly folds himself in the mantle of nonknowing. Some years ago the *Saturday Review* submitted a questionnaire to more than a score of Shakespearean directors, asking them to list the books they had found most helpful in their work.[2] A few obviously regarded books as an irrelevance; they simply looked into their hearts and directed. Members of other professions must gaze with envy upon persons so untrammeled. At the other extreme were those who obviously viewed literacy as a merit, and who had compiled imposing lists. On the whole, the results were not reassuring. Conspicuously absent was any evidence that the directors were interested in Elizabethan plays other than Shakespeare's, or in the history of trial and error in the Shakespearean theater itself. The book most often mentioned was Granville-Barker's *Prefaces,* a natural and excellent choice, but it would have been comforting if there had been more frequent mention of the kind of books Granville-Barker himself had read.

Except in the case of the authentic artist, the creative impulse tends to manifest itself in works of fancy rather than imagination. The distinction between the two made long ago by Coleridge is nowhere more graphically revealed than in the class of productions where directorial fancy is superimposed upon Shakespearean imagination. The twentieth-century break with tradition in staging methods, together with current misconceptions about the "Elizabethan manner," has often produced curious results in the use of setting and costuming. No one can question the value of freedom in these areas if used imaginatively rather than fancifully. The guiding rule would seem fairly easy to grasp—that any kind of setting and costuming (or lack of any kind) is permissible so long as the character of the play is respected. Shakespeare's plays vary considerably in their prescriptive nature: *Love's Labor's Lost* may be mounted in a wide variety of settings, whereas *Julius Caesar* and *Coriolanus,* if mounted at all, must be mounted in ancient Rome. Unfortunately, the successful mounting of *Love's Labor's Lost* elsewhere than in Renaissance Navarre, or the neutral mounting of one of the tragedies, immediately arouses rival "creativity," so that *Julius Caesar* is supplied with accouterments from Nazi Germany, the Kremlin, the Congo, or any locale not hitherto "taken." The groping for an angle or an "idea" leads to predictable permutations in successive productions—an Oriental *Lear,* an Eskimo *Lear,* a Neanderthal *Lear,* and so on.

Usually the naiveté of the "idea" betrays at once its genesis in the uncreative mind of the frustrated artist, its mechanical or fanciful quality suggesting desperation. Thus a nunnery in a play will inspire a director to invent a chorus of nuns, or a balcony in another will evoke a serenade by Negro minstrels. The presence of Spaniards in *Much Ado About Nothing* will inspire a setting in a Mexican border town, anticipating the time when *The Winter's Tale* will be set in an Alpine ski resort since Switzerland, like Bohemia, lacks a seacoast. Stunts of various kinds have always been enacted in the fringe area of the Shakespearean theater—such as the early-nineteenth-century casting of a small girl in the role of Richard III—but the fringe area in the present century has, at least sporadically, engulfed the Old Vic and the theaters erected with such high hopes in all three of the Stratfords. The primary victim is the actor, often a good one, who, whatever his instincts in the matter, is made to peer through the almond eyes of a Chinese Lear or engage in hand-to-hand combat in the way of legendary Romans while the epaulets of a Napoleonic general flap upon his shoulders. Unlike the director, he stands vulnerable and on view. A curious thing about the "novel" or "irreverent" or "daring" productions is that, once the initial flurry of publicity has subsided, even descriptions of them prove a bore. As always, embarrassment finds its balm in forgetfulness.

To shape productions to the taste of those whose interest in Shakespeare is at best ephemeral seems distinctly odd. Perhaps the best defense of the delicious "romps" and brave "renderings" that have been offered to our gaze is Machiavellian—they are calculated to irritate and cause a stir, so that, in this experimental and exploratory age, the centers sponsoring them will be advertised as sufficiently experimental and exploratory. Perhaps they are intended as salvos, with the music in the sequel. It is true that the greater number of offerings are reasonably decorous. However, it is among the less obviously eccentric productions that we find the ones which worry us most: the work of art is infiltrated rather than assaulted, and the unwary are beguiled. The director is in a position to alter details in the play, or the emphasis of the play as a whole, so that in spite of striking resemblances, the play seen is not the play billed. In the process of being made "relevant to our times," the play has ceased to be Shakespeare's and has, to a larger or smaller degree, become that of his aspiring collaborator.

There has been no age of "purity" in the treatment of Shakespeare in the theater, but the freedoms taken in the past were in one respect less licentious than those taken in the present. Whatever they did to his art, the actor-managers were respectful of Shakespeare's "message"—his sentiments and moral attitudes. They were not abashed by ideas of chastity, fidelity, patriotism, filial devotion, and the like. When they did not like what Shakespeare had done, they omitted it, and when they wished he had done something differently, they altered it, but these omissions and alterations rarely suggest ethical tampering. When they invented business in what they retained, it was to underscore rather than erase something already there. Thus, in the nineteenth century, when the Fool was reintroduced into *King Lear,* he was thrust in among the attendants in the first scene, and as he left the stage as last in the King's train, he furtively stooped and kissed the hem of Cordelia's gown. We may call this a sentimental intrusion, but it is not a falsification. In Shakespeare's play *as written* Cordelia truly deserves homage and the Fool truly adores her. In Irving's production of *The Merchant of Venice,* an idea was carried over from Verdi's *Rigoletto* and Shylock was made to re-enter after the elopement of Jessica and to stand alone and weary knocking at the door of his deserted house. Again this may be a sentimental intrusion, injurious to the balance of the play, but it too is no falsification: Shylock is truly a lonely man who has loved his home and his child. Such tricks are theatrical intensifiers, sometimes too slick or obvious, but they are less insidious than the tricks which dilute or destroy. When, in a modern production, the listeners yawn as Portia delivers her speech on mercy in languid tones, the play has been mutilated even though its text remains uncut.

The actor-managers were aware of the value of the added comic character, and they permitted the farcing of minor roles, but they limited this kind of altered coloration to characters otherwise deemed contemptible. Thus the Bishop of Winchester in *Henry VIII* was made to appear clownish, as was King Charles in *Henry V*. But they would not then, as is now habitual, convert a worthy old man like York or Gonzalo into an understudy for Polonius. Modern stereotyping is frequently perverse in more senses than one. It is interesting to see what happens to a man of fashion like Le Beau in *As You Like It*. He is drawn by Shakespeare as a time-serving but amiable courtier, and in former times made his entrance with a hunting falcon on his wrist. He now minces in with the swooping prance of the stage epicene, so that those members of the audience who would prefer to be watching a floorshow will be given their chance to laugh.

It is, or should be, the text of the play itself, and an objective reading of it, which determines comic breadth in the business. In Shakespeare's own day, the actor is said to have "almost kil'd himselfe with the scabberd"[3] when he drew his sword while playing in "The most lamentable comedy and cruel death of Pyramus and Thisbe." When Bert Lahr played Bottom recently, his comic instinct served him perfectly: he did everything ridiculous that could conceivably be done with a sword, yet kept the fun clean. In contrast a visiting academic director, on a late "lamentable" occasion, displayed his virtuosity and kinship with youth by making the playlet seem quite obscene. He would have been surprised by the private comment: the student audience knew the play and, although fond of obscenity, could not love a lie. The eighteenth and nineteenth centuries were embarrassed by Shakespeare's ribald puns, and even by some of his serious diction. The word "fornication" was permissible in the church service but not in the theater, and Shakespeare's language was universally bowdlerized. We may justly view this as a kind of negative prurience. Still, there is no superiority in positive prurience. Our theater seems less embarrassed by Shakespeare's ribaldry than by its simple character, and seems dissatisfied with the decorum of the pun. Some productions have featured a kind of "dirtiness" quite alien to the plays. Shakespearean drama is essentially cleanly, and whether or not this be deemed a virtue, one might suppose that it would now be acceptable as a novelty.

I have said that the actor-managers, even when they maimed texts by cutting and rearrangement, showed no inclination to revise Shakespeare's morals or reject his sentiments. With a few Restoration exceptions, this is true even of the more notorious adaptations. The adapter might assume that audiences would prefer "happy" to "unhappy" endings, or more obvious forms of didacticism, but never that they would be repelled by Shakespeare's romantic idealism or merely amused by his patterns of virtuous conduct. If the promptbooks prove anything, they prove that audiences were cordial to the Shakespearean ethic. The twentieth century has witnessed a revolution in sentiment, and to an undetermined degree in private morality, so that an estrangement from Shakespeare exists in some areas not unlike that which existed among the literati of the Restoration. There is more than a little hostility in the air toward Shakespeare's moral and political assumptions on the one hand and to his generous view of human nature on the other—a reaction against both his kind of conservatism and his kind of liberalism.

How extensive this alienation may be, or how permanent, no one could possibly say, but there truly exists a temptation to manipulate Shakespeare's psychological and ethical notions in the interest of others more radical, scientific, or exploratory. A director is especially vulnerable to temptation. His function is manipulative, he is offered an area in which he may exercise this function, and he naturally desires the approval of the cognoscenti. It is too much to ask that he get inside of all the characters in a play and recreate it in its own human terms; he himself is not a company of actors although he more or less governs one. The frequent result is that he superimposes upon the play he is directing some editorial idea, original or borrowed. Thus he presents not the play but a commentary upon it. For the moment at least the actor as "best commentator" yields place to the director as "sole commentator." Those of us who know how to defend ourselves against commentary, by resort to our memories or to the printed text, are not always aware of the situation of the more ingenuous playgoer, who assumes that the commentary is the play. He receives not what Shakespeare gave, but what the director thinks he should have.

Curiously the new rule that there should be no departure from the received text, except for reduction of length, proves no obstacle to manipulation. The cutting itself may be tendentious rather than merely economic, and import may be altered even when there is no cutting at all. Anything may happen when actors are directed what to do. Speeches in conflict with the chosen *idea* of the play may be thrown away or rendered self-satirizing. Business can be contrived to reverse the bearing of a whole dialogue or even an action. Actually this is more dangerous than rewriting because it encourages pride in ingenuity. The process once begun can erode away the whole substance of a play.

Let me offer in illustration the recent production of *King Lear* directed by Peter Brook. I attended a performance with a determinedly open mind. A review by Kenneth Tynan had carried the title "A World Without Gods or Hope," [4] and although the tag seemed simplistic for a work whose complexity had exercised the best critical minds of our own and the past century, a director is not responsible for his reviewers, or the reviewers for the titles given their pieces— journalism is journalism. A friend had reported to me that the King in this production was lacking in grandeur, seemed patterned upon Willy Loman, but the remark was less dampening than intended—I feel no contempt for Willy Loman. The only other eyewitness comment I had heard was a witticism about the costuming, to the effect that this was a "calf-bound" *King Lear,* but although I found the costumes indeed somewhat reminiscent of Cooper's Leatherstocking tales, so that they seemed to encourage an ostentatious virility among the ancient Britons, they were really not distracting. No conceivable production can escape censure of its details: Granville-Barker was bitterly scolded for coating Titania's train in silver.

I found a number of things to admire—the pace, the audibility and sureness of the actors, and the expertness with which a conventional stage was used. Nevertheless I sat through the performance wholly unmoved, something which had never happened to me before, although I have seen a good many far from perfect performances of this play, including two by undergraduates. Here, the trouble was the constant intrusion of the directorial *idea,* which concealed Shakespeare's play behind a series of small falsifications. The cutting was tendentious, in the interest of eliminating any amelioration of the prevailing "starkness," but this was not the gravest fault. The overall conception of a senseless universe was served by inventions which made no sense. Thus Goneril, whom Shakespeare had deprived of tear ducts along with a human heart, was made to interrupt her rejection of the father she resents to weep upon the shoulder of the husband she despises. Her charge—metaphoric, one would guilelessly suppose—that her father's train have converted her castle to a "brothel" was substantiated by a complement of appropriate inmates. By the time the male contingent had wrecked the premises, one was ready to conclude that

Goneril had acted not a moment too soon in freezing them and her father out. The weeping of the cruel daughters may have been related in some way to the this-hurts-me-more-than-it-hurts-you cliché in current domestic drama, the pangs involved in cutting the silver cord, but it functioned only as an extra bonus in misery.

"Falsification" is a hard word and should not be lightly used. To prove that I am not so using it, I must submit a very concrete detail. In the scene in which Cornwall and Regan gouge out Gloucester's eyes, Shakespeare includes three of Cornwall's servants. One of these dies trying to prevent the enormity, and he was permitted to do so in the production; no alternative was possible because the whole subsequent plot hinges upon the fatal wound he succeeds in giving Corn-wall. However, the conduct of the remaining two servants was available for manipulation. In the uncut quarto version of the play, the scene ends thus:

> 2. *Servant.* I'll never care what wickedness I do,
>   If this man comes to good.
> 3. *Servant.*   If she live long,
>   And in the end meet the old course of death,
>   Women will all turn monsters.
> 2. *Servant.* Let's follow the old Earl, and get the bedlam
>   To lead him where he would. His roguish madness
>   Allows itself to anything.
> 3. *Servant.* Go thou. I'll fetch some flax and whites of eggs,
>   To apply to his bleeding face. Now heaven help him.[5]

These lines were deleted. But then they nearly always are, and were before the folio text was printed. I am not re-cording in the present production a sin of omission but a sin of commission. The lines are included in all modern texts, and are available for anyone to see who is interested in Shakespeare's total conception. Not only were the lines omitted in the present production, but one of the servants gave the blinded man a hostile push as he groped his way from the stage.

It was not a big push. It was a small push. But all great works of art are precariously balanced, and small pushes can topple them. Or, if I may change my image, it takes only a small puff to blow out the small candle in the night, the good deed in a naughty world, which throws its light so far. I am not dealing with a triviality. Such characters as these servants come as near as anything in Shakespeare to supplying a choral voice. At this moment in the play Shakespeare is telling us that, in spite of what we have just seen, most men want to help fellow men rather than hurt them. This may or may not be true, but the fact remains that Shakespeare is saying it. To omit the statement is excusable, because it occurs in other forms in other parts of the play. But to reverse it is to betray a lack of belief in the work itself.

In front of me sat one of those clusters of young women one so often encounters at cultural events. One suspects that they are usually fellow workers in shops and offices, hungry for the "better things of life." They should be thought of as neither comic nor quaint, but the mainstay of the arts, to the disgrace of most educated males. These had obviously purchased their seats at considerable sacrifice after considerable debate. They had done so because they had heard and believed that *King Lear* is a great work of art. They were cruelly disappointed. There is nothing in the world so sad as defeated hope, the frustration of good intention, and the tragedy of the evening was enacted not on the stage but in that row of drooping girls. Shakespeare's play, if they had been permitted to see it as it is, would not have left them so empty and bewildered. If the grand *idea* of the production was indeed, as reported, borrowed from the dramas of Beckett via the criticism of Kott, and if that grand idea was the meaninglessness of life, then the production was a triumph. It was a triumph for Beckett, Kott, and Brook. It was also parasitical and fraudulent.

If I have been using strong language, it is not because of animus toward the director of this production or toward directors in general. My protest is against the kind of thing which even the ablest directors now seem to feel licensed to do. It is futile to inveigh against the directorial system. It is here, and here to stay. It is unjust too to indict directors as a class, or even particular directors unless their indiscretions are habitual. I began with a tribute to those directors who revitalized the Shakespearean theater at the turn of the present century. We owe them, and the successors who most resemble them, the fact that there is now any Shakespearean theater at all—any opportunity either for success or failure. For the first time in post-Elizabethan theatrical history it has become possible to see staged in nominally unadapted texts every one of Shakespeare's plays. The purely practical accomplishments of some of the missioners have been amazing —for instance, those of Joseph Papp, who chivalrously viewed the city multitudes as hungry for poetry and made the New York City Park Commission pretend to see eye to eye, perhaps the greatest feat in modern cultural history. Tyrone Guthrie's own Shakespearean productions have usually been deplorable both in themselves and in their influence, but he walks with giant strides, leaving theaters sprouting in his path. His rugged pioneering may be followed by civilization. Then there are those directors at the festival centers who stay more than a few years, patiently and often with inadequate means doing the best they can. Their best is often good, and no one can doubt their devotion to the drama and its greatest master.

Thus far the money that has been forthcoming in support of the classical stage has been inconsiderable compared with that which supports music and the plastic arts. It has been little money rather than big money. In the main it has been well invested. One cannot see the buses of students unloading at Stratford, Connecticut, without kindly thoughts of the men who made the center possible. One cannot see the folk waiting patiently in line to see Shakespeare in a place once so isolated as Stratford, Ontario, without being truly moved. What remains is to give these people, uncompromisingly on every occasion, the genuine thing. It is never that if it is vulgarized or perverted, and it will never do any good.

What we must keep in mind is that money is never the sole solution to anything, and that past a certain point quality cannot be purchased. The future of the Shakespearean theater depends less upon big money than upon big men. What constitutes bigness in those who mediate between the art of the past and public of the present may be hard to say. Toscanini comes to mind. It is impossible to conceive of Toscanini admitting any obligation to anything—reviewers, box office, current fashions, or this or that sector of the public—to anything except the work of art entrusted to him. When he conducted a masterpiece, only the image of the master was in his eyes.

5   THE FIERCE DISPUTE

*T*HUS FAR I have made my way with a show of assurance because my discussion has been anchored in fact. There is Elizabethan evidence about Shakespeare's life and his literary and theatrical milieu, and although we do not know all we might wish about certain matters, we know enough to form conceptions and to discuss the extent to which rival conceptions respect the existing evidence. There are fixed points of reference, firm ground for debate. We can propose a distinction between conceptions true and false—images and afterimages—and try to decide which is which. However, when we turn to the philosophical impact of a play, we find ourselves adrift. There are fixed points of reference for the impact upon later ages, but not upon Shakespeare's own. Neither he nor any of his contemporaries has left statements about what *Hamlet, Othello, King Lear,* and the rest meant to them; hence, in our quest for *meaning,* we move in a hall of mirrors where every vista recedes to a vanishing point. Nevertheless, my topic is the philosophical impact of *King Lear.*

In an age like ours, when printed commentary upon the work of an author is so abundant that several anthologies of it may be issued before the author has reached middle age, we can scarcely believe in the critical reticence of the Elizabethans. When Shakespeare died, nineteen of his works, including *King Lear,* had appeared and reappeared on the bookstalls of London, in a total of forty-seven issues. Despite this bid to the reading public by the work of the leading playwright of the age, the total printed commentary upon it amounted to little more than two thousand words—less than enough to fill one page of the *Times Literary Supplement.*

It consisted mainly of casual praise, never of interpretive criticism, and the silence on *King Lear* is absolute. Our only means of surmising what this tragedy meant to its original audience is to surmise what tragedy in general meant to it. Our points of reference are movable and dispersed.

We should not (although we usually do) accept Aristotle's conception of tragedy as a point of departure. Philip Sidney displayed some knowledge of it, probably at second hand, but no later English critic or dramatic poet until Milton displays any knowledge of it whatever. The learned Jonson and Chapman, and their admirer Webster, have left definitions of tragedy, but they never mention "the tragic flaw" or "the catharsis of fear and pity" or even the "stature" of the tragic protagonist apart from the fact that he should be of elevated social station. The Elizabethan notion of tragedy was not psychological and aesthetic, but religious and didactic, and was informed by three distinguishable ideas.[1]

Initially the conception of tragedy was inherited from the Middle Ages. A tragedy was a demonstration of the mutability of fortune and the vanity of human wishes. It showed that the greatest of men, whether virtuous or vicious, must descend ultimately to failure and death. Its message was that all men suffer and die. The idea was acceptable to Christians despite its origin in pagan pessimism because it served the doctrine that man is wise to reject this vale of tears and fix his eyes upon the world to come. This original *contemptus mundi* conception of tragedy was infiltrated during the later Middle Ages and early Renaissance by the *de casibus* conception, which was less logical but was socially more useful. Here the object was to demonstrate that the wages of sin are collected on earth—in a word, that crime does not pay. The protagonist becomes an elite malefactor, often a tyrant, who gets his just deserts. Although this idea of tragedy did not wholly supplant the older one, it dominated the thinking of

Sidney and the general theory and practice of Shakespeare's generation. The "typical" Elizabethan tragedy is non-Aristotelian because it features a criminal protagonist. Although the domestic or middle-class tragedies were more likely than "high" tragedy to introduce the motif of redemption, they were even more conspicuously moral *exampla,* dealing with such sins as adultery, available to the common man. Finally there came into elusive play the idea of tragedy as commemorative of heroic self-sacrifice, celebrating those who had died for honor, for love, for their country, or simply as the victims of an evil in which they declined to participate. Although the subject matter would normally be secular, it was inevitable in a Christian society that notes of martyrdom and atonement would be struck. We must always be alert to these notes when the suffering of the unoffending is stressed. They are more prominent in the tragedies of Shakespeare than of any other Elizabethan playwright, and are sounded explicitly in the Prologue and choral ending of *Romeo and Juliet,* his only tragedy provided with an externally stated "moral."

The three ideas of tragedy were not mutually exclusive in the sense that they defied expression except in pure form. They could interpenetrate each other in curious ways. This is why our points of reference seem constantly to shift as we discuss Elizabethan tragedy in general or any moderately complex example. Thus we can point to Lear's terrible end, quote Kent's plea that he no longer be stretched on the "rack of this tough world," and say that this is *contemptus mundi* tragedy. Or we can point to the fate of all the villains, quote Albany or Edgar on the vengeance of the gods, and say that this is *de casibus* tragedy. Or we can point to the suffering innocence of Cordelia and the chastened Lear, quote "Upon such sacrifices . . . the gods themselves throw incense," and say that this is sacrificial tragedy. But merely to conclude that the play reflects a multiple conception of tragedy is not enough. Nor should we wish to isolate particular mutually consistent details, and dishonestly define the play in their terms. If we assume that *King Lear* is a great work of art, we must assume that its lesser ideas subserve its greater idea. If we conclude that the play is predominantly tragedy of the sacrificial order, we must answer questions about the *cause* in which sacrifice is made. What is the relevance of the rite? Is the play only of interest to the comparative anthropologist and synthesizer of "myths"? Or does it say something meaningful about man's place in the universe and chance to live the good life? This is the image we are seeking.

Burbage would not have been praised in its leading role if *King Lear* had flatly failed, but it was not a great theatrical hit like *Richard III, Romeo and Juliet,* and *Hamlet.* Performance records, publication records, and the record of seventeenth-century allusions all prove that this is so. The play was less frequently mentioned than *Pericles* in the seventy-five years following Shakespeare's death, and it was acted only now and then. I have mentioned earlier that our only clue to contemporary responses is the phrase "kind Lear" in a elegy to Burbage in 1619.[2] A monosyllable of commentary is not much to go upon, but the word "kind" suggests that some positive value was seen in the Lear symbol. It was a richer word then than now, still suggesting a sense of identity with kindred and, by extension, with all human *kind.* Actually Albany applies the word to Lear in the play itself, at least in the uncut version.

For our next clue to the nature of a response we must wait for sixty years. In 1678 Elias Travers, a nonconformist chaplain of Suffolk, began recording in his Latin diary a list of his readings to the family he served. These included "Three or four Psalms . . . immediately succeeded by *King Lear,* and that again by the meditations of M. de Brieux 'On the Vanity of Human Wishes.' " [3] The amused modern discoverer of this diary remarks that "The course of reading was not a little grotesque," but it really was not so. Plainly the reverend Elias Travers was nonconformist in respect to the Establishment but not to religious tradition. *King Lear* must have struck him as a text of the *contemptus mundi* order since he utilized it as such.

In 1681 came the earliest extant piece of criticism of *King Lear,* in the dedication of Nahum Tate's altered version. [4] The alteration was undertaken, Tate tells us, in order to salvage its good things, which he described as "Lear's real and Edgar's pretended Madness" and "the Images and Language." The play is "a Heap of Jewels, unstrung and unpolisht," yet "a Treasure—none but Shakespeare could have form'd such Conceptions." Nothing is lacking but "Regularity and Probability." This may sound as if Tate was speaking as a neoclassicist offended only by structural irregularities, but his words are a trifle deceptive. He proceeds to explain that as a consequence of his efforts to provide regularity and probability he has granted "Success to the innocent distrest Persons," but obviously his primary concern was to make the play palatable. He not only arranges a marriage between Edgar and Cordelia, but rescues everyone except the villains. "Success to the innocent"—poetic justice—was not incidental but the heart of the enterprise. What this implies about the nature of his response to the original play will become clear in a moment.

Tate's version ousted Shakespeare's play from the stage for a hundred and fifty years. *King Lear* now changed from one of the least popular to one of the most popular plays in the Shakespearean repertory, played in ninety-seven of the hundred years of the eighteenth century, and standing sixth or seventh in total number of productions. [5] The success represents something more than a theatrical vagary, because the original play was widely known and the preference for the adaptation was not confined to the actor-managers and their audience. The first modern edition of Shakespeare's works, Nicholas Rowe's of 1709, was supplemented in 1710 by Charles Gildon's reprint of the *Poems* and running commentary upon the plays. Aristotle is now invoked. Tragedy, says Gildon, "by the means of Terror and Compassion, perfectly refines in us all sorts of Passions." In *King Lear*,

The King and Cordelia ought by no means to have died, and therefore Mr. Tate has very justly alter'd that Particular, which must disgust the Reader and Audience, to have Vertue and Piety meet so unjust a Reward. So that this Plot, tho of so celebrated a Play has none of the Ends of Tragedy, moving neither Fear nor Pity.[6]

In the cheap reissue of 1714 distributed by chapmen throughout the country, Gildon's judgment stands as an integral feature of Rowe's edition, so that Shakespeare's play is damned in the margin. In 1731 Thomas Cooke praised the perfection of poetic justice achieved by Tate: the wicked are punished, the virtuous rewarded, and the erring reformed; Gloucester and Lear are "placed in a State of Tranquillity and Ease agreeable to their Age and Condition."[7] Precisely how this moves us to fear and pity is not explained.

Tate, Gildon, and Cooke were small men, and might be disregarded were it not that their view was endorsed by the big men, Joseph Warton and Samuel Johnson, as well as by a long line of men and women of assorted sizes: John Dennis, Arthur Murphy, Edward Taylor, Elizabeth Griffith, William Richardson, Thomas Davies, and others, including such later redactors as Garrick, Colman, and Kemble. All were agreed that Tate had put things right where Shakespeare had gone wrong. In this contentious age, their unanimity is impressive. In 1711 Addison cast the one dissenting vote, but, as I shall point out, in a careless and unconvincing aside. He was rebuked by Dennis and said no more; thereafter his view served merely as a target for rebuttal except in one of George Steevens' sly footnotes.[8] The silences of the critics are as revealing as their statements. In 1746 John Upton argued that Shakespeare's tragedies conformed with Aristotelian precept if rightly understood; he forced *Hamlet, Othello,* and *Macbeth* into the procrustean bed, but fought shy of *King Lear.*[9] Thomas Edwards, Elizabeth Montagu, and Thomas Francklin praised details in the play, but remained reticent on the central issue, the propriety of its ending.[10] It was safe to trace the course of Lear's distraction and praise it as "natural." Toward the end of the era the vocabulary of criticism was expanding, and such matters as sublimity, sympathy, and imagination were stressed. There were volumes like Richard Payne Knight's *Principles of Taste,* 1805, where *King Lear* would seem perfect for use as illustration. Shakespeare's other tragedies are used, but not this one: it remains a stone rejected by the builder.

It is easy to grow contemptuous of this body of criticism, but we should be cautious in doing so. In some ways it shows more consistency and honesty than some of our own. The critics had the advantage of living in an age when it was still possible to believe that Shakespeare might occasionally err. They did not apply neoclassical rules mechanically. Garrick even considered restoring the Fool expunged by Tate, providing the actor would "promise to be very chaste in his colouring, and not to counteract the agonies of Lear."[11] The critics display no spiritual aridity or dearth of feeling. Audiences broke into "loud lamentations" at Lear's distresses and would have been devastated by Shakespeare's ending. They preferred Tate's version to the original, but did not confuse the two. Although they craved the comfort of "poetic justice," they did not falsely create it in the original play by loading Cordelia with fancied guilt or magnifying the guilt of Lear. They read the original play attentively to its end, and saw that it was a Lear presumably redeemed who was submitted to the final agony—and this, as Johnson complained, without the authority of the chronicles. They saw that Lear's spirit of resignation does not survive this agony, since he enters howling, curses the bystanders, and rejects the dispensation of the gods: "Why should a dog, a horse, a rat have life? And thou no breath at all." They did not construe his retreat into illusion—"See there, she lives!"—as a beatific vision. They elected to approve Tate's version rather than to Tatefy the original play with apologetic criticism.

So far as I know, there was no questioning of Shakespeare's truths. Warton takes refuge by quoting Boileau, "Le vrais peut quelquefois n'être pas vraisemblable," [12] and Edward Taylor by endorsing a modicum of endearing falsehood, "let the delusion be on the side of virtue, that I may still flatter myself with the pleasing belief, that to be good is to be happy." [12] Doctor Johnson concedes that it may be a "just representation" but lets his sentiments confirm the "general suffrage" that the last scenes are too shocking to be endured. [14] He himself could write somberly on the vanity of human wishes, but was disinclined to be tossed ruthlessly upon simple reliance on faith by anything so unexpected as a stage play. The idea that Shakespeare was preaching stoic fortitude was properly rejected. Addison had quoted Seneca, "A virtuous Man ... struggling with Misfortunes is such a Spectacle as Gods might look upon with Pleasure." He had praised the sentiments of Corneille and Racine, and listed *King Lear* with an odd assortment of tragedies including *Oedipus Rex* and *Oroonoko*. [15] No one could accept such a context as appropriate for Shakespeare's play, or think of Lear, the least resigned of all tragic heroes, as a kind of British Cato. Hume's statement of the purpose of tragedy, "to express a noble courageous despair,"[16] seemed equally inapplicable, especially since he designated as improper to tragedy "such horrible subjects as Crucifixions and Martyrdoms." Abroad Schiller was the chief theorizer about tragedy, and he too demanded a stoic hero or a morally purposive one. He could accept Coriolanus, but not Lear, who seemed to him to be too weak and foolish even to inspire strong pity.[17] The critic appears to allow Aristotle to dictate his emotional response.

The eighteenth century had no theory of tragedy which would shelter *King Lear*. We are now in a position to deduce what their image of the play was. Shunning the rigors of the *contemptus mundi* mode, they preferred to view the play as a moral *exemplum* in which the distribution of rewards and punishments badly needed straightening out. Since the play did not seem to offer a benign purgative of the emotions, it was not Aristotelian. Since its hero had no ethical program or emotional self-control, it was not Stoic. Since it offered no closed demonstration of merciful redemption and the justice of the gods, it was not a theodicy with Christian implications. In its original form it could neither profit nor delight. The common sense of the age bespoke devotion to comfort and utility. The lighter modes of literature should delight morally, while the serious modes should moralize delightfully. The benevolent emotions which Shaftesbury had associated with actual suffering and practical humanitarianism were transferred to the realm of aesthetic enjoyment. Mrs. Montagu speaks of tender pity as the proper effect of tragedy, "to touch the heart" and "mend it."[18] Moral and religious orthodoxy was put to pleasurable use, with sanctions sought in the doctrine of catharsis. What was really wanted in tragedy was safe excitement, sensations of benevolence, and pleasantly moderate woe.

The Germans had been too preoccupied with *Hamlet* to devote much attention to *King Lear,* and the fragmentary comment they produced before Schlegel shows no illumination. Schlegel's critique of 1808 was more sympathetic than anything that had been produced either in England or abroad thus far. His summing up of the message of the play is an oblique concession to the *contemptus mundi* concept: "The persons of this drama have only such a faint belief in Providence as heathens may be supposed to have; and the poet wishes to show us that this belief requires a wider range than the dark pilgrimage on earth to be established in its utmost extent." Of Lear he says that the "rays of a high and kingly disposition burst forth from the eclipse of his understanding." In reference to the Tate version current in England, he says:

After surviving so many sufferings, Lear can only die in a tragical manner from his grief for the death of Cordelia; and if he is also to be saved and pass the remainder of his days in happiness, the whole loses its signification.[19]

For this pronouncement, Schlegel deserves our admiration and gratitude. It anticipates by four years the following by Charles Lamb:

A happy ending!—as if the living martydrom that Lear had gone through,—the flaying of his feelings alive, did not make a fair dismissal from the stage of life the only decorous thing for him. If he is to live and be happy after, if he could sustain this world's burdens after, why all this pudder and preparation,—why torment us with all this unnecessary sympathy? As if the childish pleasure of getting his gilt robes and sceptre again could tempt him to act over again his misused station,—as if at his years, and with his experience, anything was left but to die.[20]

To say that the idea of the two passages is the same is a little misleading. By his fervor, his choice of language, and his invoking of emotional rather than rational necessities—why otherwise "torment us with all this unnecessary sympathy?" —Lamb has transformed the idea.

It was indeed Lamb who turned the tide of *Lear* criticism. His "Essay on the Tragedies of Shakespeare," published in the *Reflector* in 1812, is a landmark in the history of criticism. It took its polemical form because of the adaptations of Shakespeare current in the theaters of the time, but its paradoxical thesis, that the plays are unsuitable for the stage, should not deflect attention from its true theme—the symbolic dimension of the tragic heroes. After his indignant rejection of the idea of a "tottering old man" to whom we may condescend, he gets to the root of the matter:

The greatness of Lear is not in corporal dimension, but in intellectual: the explosions of his passion are terrible as a volcano: they are storms turning up and disclosing to the bottom that sea his mind, with all its vast riches. It is his mind which is laid bare. This case of flesh and blood seems too insignificant to be thought on; even as he himself neglects it. On the stage we see nothing but corporal infirmities and weakness, the impotence of rage; while we read it, we see not Lear, but we are Lear,—we are in his mind, we are sustained by a grandeur which baffles the malice of daughters and storms; in the aberrations of his reason, we discover a mighty irregular power of reasoning, immethodized from the ordinary purposes of life, but exerting its powers, as the wind blows where it listeth, at will upon the corruptions and abuses of mankind.[21]

This is fine, making us realize that fine criticism like fine poetry must issue from heart as well as mind.

Incredible as it seems, it is in Lamb's essay that a great work of art, already two hundred years old, receives for the first time on record unstinted and unqualified praise. Specifically, Lamb does three things which had not been done before. He shows no fastidious detachment: "we see not Lear, but we are Lear." Second, he lets those "rays of a high and kingly disposition" seem more than incidental: Lear is a great protagonist, a figure of "grandeur." And third, mainly by his choice of words, he invests this figure with sacrificial robes: Lear endures "living martyrdom" in the "flaying of his feelings alive" as he opposes his valiant anger against "the corruptions and abuses of mankind." Lamb's predecessors could not think of sacrificial figures as conducting themselves with Lear's lack of decorum or well-defined social mission. Lamb himself did not really think about the matter. He is not explicit about the *meaning* of Lear's suffering; rather, by his intense and sympathetic partisanship, he intimates what he feels.

The Elizabethan theater was a secular institution in a religious age, and the laws discouraged anything but the most formal and conventional type of expression in matters of doctrine; "religious" plays as such are rare. On the other hand, there was no strict partition in the Elizabethan mind between religious and other areas of concern. Lamb, and his immediate associates Hazlitt and Keats, by very reason of their heterodoxy, were able to restore religious sentiment to secular contexts. After Lamb's use of the term "living martyrdom," similar tropes begin to appear in comment on *King Lear*. In a review of Campbell's *Specimens* published in *Blackwood's* in 1819, we hear of the "indestructible divinity of the spirit" [22] of the one who not long before had been patronizingly pitied. The critic makes due acknowledgment to Lamb. A few years earlier, Hazlitt had ended an essay on the play with a mixture of spiritual and nautical tropes, and a long quotation from Lamb. Hazlitt sometimes viewed tragedy as a gladiatorial spectacle, atavistic in appeal, sometimes as the very reverse, just as his view of human nature fluctuated between fear of the worst and hope for the best. Unlike Lamb, he was interested in the theory of catharsis, which he usually equates with moral purification and growth. He does so in essays on *Othello* and *King Lear*: tragedy, he says, gives us a "high and permanent interest in

humanity as such ... It makes one a partaker with his kind."
Hazlitt saw Lear as a champion partaker. He is thinking of
Lear's initial faith in humanity when he speaks of his
imagination being "wrenched from all its accustomed holds
and resting places in the soul," and this faith is the deep-
bedded "anchor" of Lear the storm-lashed "ship."[23] The
image is confused but heroic. Hazlitt considered *King Lear*
the greatest of all tragedies, and communicated that belief to
Keats.

We have Keats's copy of Hazlitt's *Characters of Shakespear's Plays* (1817) and only the chapter on *King Lear*
contains underscorings and marginalia. Keats seems principally interested in the matter of "poetic intensity," which
he associates with philosophical import. In a letter to his
brothers on December 21, 1817, he writes of the play as illustrating how great art in its intensity makes "all disagreeables
evaporate" and excites "momentous depth of speculation."[24]
A month later he wrote his sonnet "On Sitting Down to
Read King Lear Once Again." It describes a process of
cleansing immolation which brings new strength and creativity:

> ... once again the fierce dispute
> Betwixt damnation and impassion'd clay
> Must I burn through; once more humbly assay
> The bitter-sweet of this Shakespearean fruit.

Keats's letters let us gloss the word "bitter-sweet" and thus
trace the direction of the speculation stirred in his mind by
the play. On the day after he composed the sonnet, he mentions in a letter to Bailey that he had written on *King Lear*
because he so "felt the greatness of the thing." The letter
contains a passage relating to a quite different subject but
evoking an image of "impassion'd clay":

... there lives not the Man who may not be cut up, aye hashed to
pieces on his weakest side. The best of Men have but a portion

of good in them—a kind of spiritual yeast in their frames which creates the ferment of existence—by which a Man is propell'd to act and strive and buffet with Circumstance.[25]

A few weeks later in a letter to Reynolds the "spiritual yeast" reappears as the "mould ethereal" in one of the most famous passages in Keats. By communication of the portion of good "every human might become great" and humanity be transformed from a briary heath to a "grand democracy of Forest Trees."[26] During the year following, darkened by successive personal catastrophes, Keats was in need of a faith. The part played by *King Lear* in his search is suggested in a journal-letter to George Keats and his wife in America, in an entry dated April 21, 1819. It begins, "The whole appears to resolve into this—that Man is originally 'a poor forked creature' . . ." Keats is remembering Lear's address to the Tom o' Bedlam, who is "naked and near to beast"—"unaccommodated man is no more but such a poor, bare, forked animal as thou art"—followed by Lear's mighty question: "Is man no more than this?" After disclaiming belief in human perfectibility, Keats unexpectedly states a creed:

The common cognomen of this world among the misguided and superstitious is "a vale of tears" from which we are to be redeemed by a certain arbitrary interposition of God and taken to Heaven— What a little circumscribed straightened notion! Call the world if you Please "The vale of Soul-making." Then you will find out the use of the world . . .[27]

The youthful bravado with which Christian doctrine is here misconceived and dismissed should not obscure the religious character of what follows, called by Keats "a faint sketch of a system of salvation." It allegorizes a process by which "atoms of perception . . . sparks of divinity" assume identity as souls through suffering. It is the poet's justification of the ways of God, working through men rather than upon them.

Although the terminology is far from scientific, the thought is not far removed from that expressed in our own day in Teilhard de Chardin's *Phenomenon of Man*.

We may dismiss everything but a few suggestive phrases— "living martyrdom," "fierce dispute betwixt damnation and impassion'd clay," "vale of soul-making"—and still be aware that these new spokesmen see Lear as a symbol of sacrifice in the cause of man's struggle against brutishness. "Is man no more than this?" The questioner is accepted as the answer to his own question. Man is more than this because of men like Lear, the fierce disputant; he is clay but within his frame is the "spiritual yeast" which "creates the ferment of existence." He symbolizes man's redeeming hunger for a state distinct from beast's, and man's willingness to pay the price in pain. Whatever we think of the conception, we must be impressed by its spontaneity. It was doubtless influenced by the stirrings of evolutionary thought, organicism, the view of life as process, but mainly it was the fruit of simple receptiveness. It owed nothing to a self-perpetuating critical and theatrical tradition. The play was seen afresh, much as if it had been new, and was accepted as it is, without rejections or rationalizations. It was seen whole, with everything in it viewed in relation to the central symbol of Lear, so that Cordelia could claim admiration without deflecting attention from the theme. It would be presumptuous of us to speak airily of the "romanticism" of sensibilities which recovered a work of art. Through the strength of their conviction, the "romantics" drove Tate's substitute version from the stage. It is not often that criticism can point to accomplishments so concrete. When Dickens reviewed Macready's production of the restored *King Lear* in 1838,[28] one can still detect in his fine essay echoes of the words of Lamb.

For the remainder of the nineteenth century the idea of sacrificial tragedy tended to color commentary rather than shape it. The best commentary of the eighteenth century had been that which analyzed the psychology of Lear and affirmed its "naturalness." This kind persisted—inevitably, since Lear is at once the greatest metaphor of the play and its most realistic character. The realism, the persuasive "touches of nature," continued to serve as invitation. Coleridge's remarks, although not published until 1836–1839, were made in lectures delivered in precisely the period, 1812–1819, when Lamb, Hazlitt, and Keats were recording their conception, and his remarks compared with theirs have an eighteenth-century cast;[29] his method of mingling psychological and ethical observations proved less suitable to this play than to any of the others. In 1848 the neglected American critic, H. N. Hudson, wrote subtly on the motives which may have prompted Lear's abdication of power, demand for professions of love, and rejection of Cordelia.[30] The influence of Lamb is chiefly perceptible in Hudson's impulse to exonerate Lear. No one was content any longer simply to call him weak and foolish, or to analyze his mental malady.

Until the time of Bradley's famous lectures of 1904, and to some extent since, the concentration upon *characters* as the center of interest has fostered a tendency to see the message of a play as a message to some character within it. This is not quite the same thing as seeing the play as a whole as a message to us. Dowden escaped the hazard by really carrying out the common resolution to speak of the Lear symbol with humble brevity. He spoke in general terms of "suffering humanity" and the "purifying ordeal"[31]—we wish he had said more. We may wish that Bradley had said a little less. He said certain true things better than they had ever been said before, but he diminished the play by proposing as its title "The Redemption of King Lear."[32] To particularize thus, as he and others have done, about Lear's redemption, or salvation, or learning the lesson of humility, is to postulate sensations of aloofness which we do not feel, and to find signposts in the ending which are not there. Lear does not behave penitently at the very end, and we do not feel like requiring him to do so. The punishment he has received is in such excess of his offenses that we have long since dismissed the bill of particulars against him. If we say that he has learned the lesson of humility, we must explain by what easier means we have attained the humility authorizing us to lay a diploma on his bier. Shakespeare has forced us to withdraw our gaze from Lear's faults and to fix it on the mitigating circumstances, primarily his high evaluation of love, from which his faults derive. He effects this shift in focus by making Lear's suffering the greatest reality in the play, so that at the end we can see and feel little else. Since we refuse at the last to judge him, it is we who have been converted. The play achieves its ends by artistic indirection.

Although Lear is indeed an individual, we are compelled to see him as something more. We return to Keats's "vale of soul-making." The phrase keeps recurring in twentieth-century criticism of *King Lear,* usually without notice that Keats himself had made the connection. The idea spreads that Shakespeare's play deals with the growth of the soul of mankind, rather than of a particular man. Religious terminology is common in this criticism. In 1930 G. Wilson Knight used as his keyword for the play "purgatorial" [33]—in a general not specific sense. In 1939 R. W. Chambers cited in association with it the death of Socrates and the "man of sorrows" in Second Isaiah, who "by his knowledge justifies many"—he quotes the Book of Wisdom: "as gold in the furnace has he tried them and received them as a living offering." [34] In 1948 H. B. Charlton wrote, "A spiritual civilization is dimly emerging and man is making or discovering a morality. But the price of it is heavy in blood and tears; and the picture of Lear paying this price is the main stuff of the drama."[35] In 1951 Arthur Sewell spoke thus: "For Lear the world is indeed a 'vale of soul-making.' And the making of a soul is the transformation of man's universe as well as of man himself.... Lear's madness gives us a glimpse of Chaos; and it gives us the hope, too, that out of such Chaos, as by a transubstantiation, Blessedness is somehow born."[36] The tragedy, he continues, moves "towards the vision of a kind of identity which comes to men when they are members of each other" and escape "a beastly and self-destructive individualism."[37] This is the fashion in which thoughtful critics now define "the bitter-sweet of this Shakespearean fruit."

We must admit that a mystery remains. Lear himself dies without a glimpse of the light shed by the critics. Redemption is conferred upon him by a critical act of faith. Perhaps this is the most significant if least conscious feature of the doctrine of Bradley and his followers. Many have spoken of the "mystery" of the play—Dowden of its "grand inexplicableness,"[38] Bradley of its "mystery we cannot fathom,"[39] and Charlton of the "sense of inscrutable mysteries."[40] *King Lear* is a play about love, and its mystery, I believe, attaches itself primarily to the nature of love, and this in turn to the paradox of the redeemer unredeemed.

Much has been said about the improbability of the opening situation, but perhaps not enough about the greatest improbability in it—that an ancient man, fourscore and upward, and every inch a king, should value love so much. Has he not ceased long since to care? The intensity of his concern is psychologically so incredible that Coleridge attempted to rationalize it into a species of tyranny derived from "inveterate habits of sovereignty,"[41] and Freud by making it tantamount to an aged man's proper preoccupation with death.[42] But Coleridge, in conceding that Lear's "selfishness" was that of "a loving and kindly nature," merely described the paradox he was attempting to resolve. "Selfish" love is a contradiction in terms. Love like truth is an absolute, which we cannot define although we know it exists, and which we cannot modify except to destroy. For Lear love is a reality. The dimension of his initial "selfishness" or "folly," like the dimension of his later suffering is the measure of the value he places upon love. The play leaves us in no doubt that it is the thing itself he values, and not the practical advantages accruing from it. Sacrificial tragedy is concerned with those who value things not as they *are* but as they *should be* valued; and there is something of Lear in most of Shakespeare's tragic heroes. They could save themselves at any moment by the simple expedient of behaving credibly, in a fashion "true to life." Most of them die on the cross of their excessive human attachments. Lear is the most heroic. He affirms the reality and value of love until the moment his heart bursts.

But while there can be no question that he loves, there is a question of a different kind. Why does he think that love is denied him? The play portrays three of the most loving characters to be found in literature anywhere, Cordelia, Kent, and the Fool, whom Hudson called "a hero in motley." [43] The focus of their love is Lear, and there is never a moment in the play when one or another of them is far from his side. Kent is beseeching his attention as he kneels by Cordelia's body. Lear dies craving the thing he has always had. It is in this sense that he dies unredeemed: he has *not* learned. An aura of martyrdom surrounds him because his suffering stems from the value he has placed on a thing of value, but he dies a martyr without faith. Still, and the point cannot be too much stressed, the ending leaves us in no mood for censure. Our own capacity for love is being probed. Throughout Cordelia has commanded our love for what she is, and Lear has implored it for what he needs. So far as we are capable of submitting one, our judgment is that no greater symbols have been offered anywhere of man's capacity for love, and need to love and be loved.

Perhaps the resolution of the paradox of the redeemer unredeemed—the reason why, in the grand design of the play, Lear must appear as both martyred and dying in imperfection—is that there are two Lears in the play. There is the particular human being, a father who loses a beloved child by his own fault, recovers her, and then loses her again forever. His anguish enters into us like an ache, and whatever the limitations of his love, we feel that he has at least loved something more than we have ever loved anything: the question of his personal redemption is not submitted to us. And then there is Lear as Humanity figure, incorporating this erring, loving, suffering individual. In his aspect as Humanity figure, Lear cannot end the course redeemed because the Humanity he symbolizes is not redeemed.

At the end of the play, the nation is purged of its manifest evil, and social order is restored. In this respect *King Lear* conforms with the Shakespearean formula, and it is wanton to maintain that its simple preachment is despair or that its maker has lapsed into pessimism. As a matter of fact, when Albany addresses Edgar and Kent,

> Friends of my soul, you twain,
> Rule in this realm, and the gored state maintain,

we witness, as we do not in any of the other tragedies except possibly *Macbeth,* power passing into the hands of the morally fit rather than the casually convenient. If we were to compare Albany, Kent, and Edgar with Fortinbras, Antony, Octavius, Aufidius, Montano, and those other worldlings who succeed to power in the other tragedies, we would have to conclude that here is Shakespeare's "happiest" ending. But it is natural that we do not do so. There is no elation in

the voice of anyone—all is still "cheerless, dark, and deadly."
The poetry tells us that the real war is not yet over.

Critics have noted the inconclusiveness of the conclusion—
Richard Sewell when he says that all it does is to "keep the
future open to possibility,"[44] Arthur Sewell when he says
that it poses the question, "What shall we do to be saved?"[45]
The impression that it deals with a process rather than an
end product is reinforced by the impression that the action
proceeds outside of time. Its "primitivism" is a superficial
feature. J. C. Maxwell's statement that it is "a Christian play
about a pagan world"[46] would be equally true if reversed:
it is a pagan play about a Christian world, so far as there
yet exists any Christian world for it to be about. Since
evolution involves temporal progression, the process we witness seems not evolutionary in an historical or scientific
sense. We do not see Lear achieving humanity as he extri-
cates himself from a world of brutes. Rather we see him as
a symbol in a world of symbols, some good and some evil.
At the beginning of the play there are symbols of love of a
purity which Lear's own love never achieves. Again we are
reminded of *The Phenomenon of Man,* where "psycho-
genesis" (soul making) is viewed as the creation of the pre-
existing through the agency of what Keats had called "sparks
of divinity."

Religious terminology and the invocation of "mystery"
are inevitable in *Lear* criticism because the play makes us
look at and beyond mankind. It seems to say that everything
depends upon what men do, and yet to say that men cannot
do all. We are forced to ask if "human love" in the world
of nature can be anything more than an alloy—if there can
be such a thing as "human love" unfed by love of some other
kind. What is the ultimate referent for all our fine words
and phrases? Can there be belief in universal brotherhood

without belief in universal fatherhood, belief in humanity without belief in divinity—indeed, belief in anything without belief in God? And yet God is not a distinguishable presence in the play. Instead there are other worldly forces addressed fearfully or hopefully as gods. The play does not answer the religious question, but it forces us inexorably to ask it.

Shakespeare did not compose the play as a metaphysical exercise and consciously create its "mystery." He could not have answered its questions, perhaps could not even have asked them in any other way. But there was an image in his eye. The one thing we can agree upon is that it is an image which greatly concerns us. *King Lear* may be Shakespeare's divine comedy which we are still striving to learn to read.

RELATED ESSAYS

6 SHAKESPEARE AS CULTURE HERO

*A*NTI-STRATFORDIANS, mistaking brevity for evasive-ness, have often charged that scholars of the "estab-lishment" refuse to meet their arguments. Their grounds of complaint must surely have been removed in recent years; a surprising number of works have appeared submitting the various authorship claims to sober examination.[1] The analysts sometimes betray amusement with the material with which they must deal, but the tone of their works has been in general detached and nonpolemical. In view of this new and sagacious tendency, we can look forward perhaps to an ultimate his-torical evaluation of the movement to displace Shakespeare— a work addressed to the problem, not of whether he wrote his plays, but of why there have been persistent claims that he did not. So far as the present essay has any serious inten-tion, it is to open a discussion of the philosophical, or at least the sociological and psychological, basis of the controversy.

We must admit, I think, that the Shakespearean case is virtually unique. Peculiar cults have attached themselves transiently to Dante, Cervantes, and other great writers, but doubts about their claims to their own works have never persisted. Among the English poets, Chaucer, Spenser, Jon-son, and a number more were just as humble in social origins as Shakespeare, but they have been left in undisputed poses-sion of their works, except where the Baconian and Ox-fordian claims have expanded. Almost the entire literary output of the Renaissance, at home and abroad, was finally claimed for Bacon by his adherents; but this is only a by-product of the anti-Shakespearean impulse, not a separate phenomenon. Only skeletal biographies exist of most of the old writers; in fact, we have as a rule less information about them than about Shakespeare, and we must wonder why his activities alone have been subjected to such furious debate.

It is dangerous to say categorically that the doubters are faddists and snobs. The anti-Shakespearean movement is different from other fads (such, for instance, as belief in the water cure, perpetual motion, or the ouija board), both in its durability and in the kind of people associated with it. Though many of these skeptics have been obviously eccentric, many others have not. A considerable number have been expert in their own specialties and sensible in their everyday lives. Usually they do not, like the typical faddist, flit from one enterprise to another; attacking Shakespeare is their one true cause, and they are often willing to devote to it time, energy, and money, as well as to defy ridicule. This last is especially significant. Although happily they are not required to shed it, there runs in their veins the blood of the martyrs.

All stock explanations of the recurring hostility toward the man from Stratford must be dismissed as inadequate. The typical anti-Shakespearean book begins by repeating something long disproved but still held to as an article of faith—that the Shakespeares were illiterates in a backward community. It proceeds to illustrate that Bacon, or Oxford, or whoever the candidate may be (and the list ranges from Christopher Marlowe, M.A., to Queen Elizabeth herself) was highly educated and superbly versed in the law, music, hunting, courtly manners, and all the other subjects with which the author of the plays was so obviously conversant. It concludes with a piecing together of dark clues, ciphers, and so on, proving that here is the true author revealed at last. Now the reasoning processes thus displayed are so defective, and the conclusions reached so beyond the gullibility range of the average literate person, that we are apt to attribute any favorable response to certain common human foibles. First, we might cite the naive or innocent response, based on a trust of all statements in print: if Shakespeare was illiterate and the other candidate literate, surely the latter is the more likely author. Second, the conditioned response, induced by a combination of simple repetition (so effective in other forms of propaganda) with the thesis of detective fiction: since the Watsons of the world see only obvious evidence, it is safer to put one's money on Sherlock Holmes. Third, the malicious response, reflecting a cynical fondness for exposure literature, "confidential" or other, regardless of its injustice in particular cases. Fourth, and far different, the chivalrous or sentimental response: the book is backing a dark horse in defiance of the stuffy professors. Now while these four common human reactions (and I am omitting "snob appeal," since it is, or should be, canceled out by democratic sentiment) may indeed operate in some measure and explain the casual approval of each new candidate by some sector of the public, they do not explain enough. They do not explain why both old and new claims have flourished for more than a century and have attracted men who in other connections are not naive, sentimental, malicious, or conditioned by repetitive techniques and types of popular fiction.

We must look for the deeper appeal of these books and the movement they represent, and I think we find it in something that the readers themselves do not always recognize— the lure of the mystical. The authors are, in their own way, mystics, and the spurious mystery with which they deal is subtended by a sense of real mystery of a semireligious character. For instance, resurrection is a common motif in these books, or something resembling resurrection. Bacon is given works written after his death. Nearly all of the works were written after Marlowe's recorded death. Elizabeth died in 1603 and Oxford in 1604, whereas Shakespearean plays continued to be written until 1613. The authors do not actually invoke the miraculous in explaining away these discrepancies, but miracles seem hovering in the wings.

Now the idea of resurrection is a constant one in connection with what anthropologists call "culture heroes." Culture heroes are legendary figures who appear with common characteristics in all human societies. They are huge mythical symbols, variously conceived of as kings, sages, or gods—the conquerors and lawgivers of the tribe. They may or may not have their point of departure in actual outstanding men, whose historical identities have been completely replaced by myth. King Arthur, for instance, is a culture hero, and scholars are still divided over the nature of the sprout from which his story grew. But, according to that story, he lies even now in some British cavern awaiting the day of his resurrection.

The idea suggests itself that what has actually happened in the case of Shakespeare is that his high repute for wisdom has triggered a mythmaking process such as has operated many times before in human cultures and that the solution to the puzzling aspects of the Shakespeare controversy lies in works which have nothing to do with Shakespeare, such as Lord Raglan's *The Hero* (first published in 1936)[2] or Otto Rank's *The Myth of the Birth of the Hero* (1914).[3] We must inquire into the general process of mythmaking, and its basis in human psychology. When we do this, the Shakespearean case reveals so many points of kinship with recognized examples of the process that we wonder why the cultural anthropologists have not hit upon it. Possibly it is because they have assumed that the creation of culture heroes can occur only in primitive societies.

But let us look at the Shakespearean case in its general outlines. Shakespeare, as even the Baconians concede, was a living man, whose birth, marriage, death, whereabouts, possessions, and acting career are mentioned in contemporary documents. But these ordinary facts seemed increasingly inadequate as the extraordinary nature of his accomplishments became manifest, and they began to be pieced out with myth. Lord Raglan estimates that the process of mythmaking begins about fifty years after the subject's death, when his mark remains, but his person is fading from memory. About fifty years after Shakespeare's death, there was no written biography available, but his mark was visible indeed: his works were about to go into their third edition, playhouse managers were competing for rights to perform his plays, and three successive poets-royal[4]—Jonson, Davenant, and Dryden—had hailed him as a nonpareil. A story now became current that he was driven from Stratford by Sir Thomas Lucy for poaching his deer.[5] Scholars point out that Lucy possessed no deer park and the story seems unlikely; but it is otherwise identifiable as myth, combining as it does two traditional motifs usually associated with culture heroes— that of his turbulent behavior in youth and that of the persecutor who hounds him into exile. In other words the process of transformation has begun.

In the eighteenth century most of the recorded facts about Shakespeare were assembled, but they were unimpressive compared with his swelling reputation. His plays were the staple of the only legitimate theaters and could boast as their editors Rowe, another poet laureate, Pope, the greatest poet, Johnson, the greatest pundit, and Malone, the greatest scholar of the age. Learned men were disputing about the author's learning. The classical scholar Dr. Francklin was conceding that Aeschylus, Sophocles, and Euripides were only approximately of Shakespeare's stature;[6] and the nation in general was pitting him as its champion against the poets of rival France.

The next step in mythmaking was bound to come. Its

nature requires a foreword of explanation. There are heroes of history, heroes of myth, and heroes in between like Alexander the Great. The known facts about heroes of history, their births, deaths, and accomplishments, form no perceptible pattern except that their accomplishments are greater than normal and their deaths often more violent. No mystery ordinarily attends their births, and they are recognized as the natural children of their presumed parents. With the heroes of myth—the culture heroes—the case is different. Their careers follow a distinctive pattern, and one of the most amazing facts in cultural history is the uniformity of this pattern whenever and wherever the hero emerges—in ancient Babylon or Israel, Egypt or Iceland, Homeric Greece or medieval Germany, India or England, Mexico or central Africa. We are concerned only with the detail of the pattern relating to the hero's birth. The salient fact is that a mystery attends it, a problem of identity: he is never the person he appears to be.

Everyone is familiar with this feature of the pattern as reflected in folklore, fairy tales, and romances. The child is distinguished from the peasants who appear to be its parents, a girl by her beauty and charm, a boy by his cleverness and courage, until the girl proves to be a princess or the boy a prince. The duckling is really a swan. Or we are familiar with it in the legends of our own culture. Who was King Arthur— the son of the duke of Cornwall or of Uther Pendragon? Who was Robin Hood—the son of a Saxon yeoman or of Robert, earl of Huntington?

In the myth of the birth of the hero there is always the initial mystery. At the very dawn of human history Sargon of Babylon was reared by Akki, the humble water carrier, but he was really the son of a vestal and became the king of Agade or Akkad. Karna, the Hindu epic hero, was reared by a mere charioteer but was the son of Princess Pritha by Surya the sun god. Karkhrosov of Persia was reared by herdsmen but was the son of Princess Feringis. King Cyrus, also the apparent son of herdsmen, was really the child of Princess Maridane of the Medes. Siegfried was reared by the blacksmith, Mimur, but was the son of the Princess Sisibe. Tristram was the son of the Princess Blanchefleur, not of Rual and his wife who reared him. Moses was the son of true Levites, not of the Egyptian foster mother who found him in the bulrushes. The Greek gods, demigods, and chieftains have usually a mysterious birth, or deceptive identity, and were reared away from their true parents—even Zeus, Apollo, and Dionysus. Paris was reared by shepherds on Mount Ida though he was a prince of Troy, Jason reared by Cheiron though the son of King Aeson. Frequently the supposed father was merely a human stand-in for a god, as in the case of Pelops, Perseus, Theseus, Telephus, Romulus, Bellerophon, Asclepius, Herakles, Ion, and others. Ambiguities of origin often make it hard to distinguish the culture hero in his three possible roles—as lineal king or high priest, mighty conqueror, or god, as in the case of Quetzalcoatl of Mexico, Nyikang of the upper Nile, Horus of Egypt, and Attis of Asia. A hero like Alexander was indubitably historical, but in the process of subsequent magnification he acquired a miraculous birth.

Now England's great poet was called Shakespeare, but he could not really have been Shakespeare. Shakespeare was reared by tradesfolk of Stratford, but England's great poet must really be Sir Francis Bacon, Lord Verulam, Viscount St. Albans, the omniscient lord chancellor of the realm. In view of the other circumstances propitious to mythmaking, this amalgam was bound to occur, and it occurred on schedule. Shakespeare had grown too big to be encompassed by a certain type of imagination unless reshaped as a culture hero. How complete this reshaping has been and to what extent it follows a standard pattern has been obscured by the fact that our attention has shifted from the Baconians to the Oxfordians and other rival sects. But let us keep our eye for the moment on the Baconians. We do not know when minds first became receptive to the idea of deceptive identity in the national poet-hero, but the first man on record to communicate his conviction that Shakespeare was Bacon was the Reverend James Wilmot in about the year 1781.[7] The movement stayed underground, making only fitful appearances until the middle of the nineteenth century, when it found its prophet and martyr in the American sage Delia Bacon. The last decades of the century and the first of the next were the period of its greatest spread, when even national figures like Bismarck and Lord Palmerston announced their conversion. Regular societies were founded, and periodicals issued as well as a deluge of books.

More interesting for diagnostic purposes are the years that followed, after the public clamor subsided and Baconianism passed into the keeping of the true devotees, where it now resides. These have proceeded to prove that the same great spirit created not only the works of Shakespeare and Bacon, but also those of Spenser and other English authors as late as the eighteenth century, as well as those of Montaigne, Cervantes, and other foreigners. Furthermore, they have collectively agreed that Bacon was not really Bacon, but was in fact the son of Queen Elizabeth. This, too, was predictable. Among the culture heroes whose careers have been analyzed and collated by Lord Raglan, such figures as Theseus, Romulus, Herakles, Perseus, Asclepius, Dionysus, Apollo, and Llew Llawgiffin of Wales all prove to be the sons of royal virgins, and there are more besides. Most of us still think of Elizabeth I as the Virgin Queen, and we can understand the emotional appeal of this final phase of Baconianism; but since it has developed in a naturalistic age, Elizabeth's royalty is accepted but her virginity subjected to doubt. Bacon was the son not of his supposed father but of Elizabeth's favorite, the earl of Leicester. A typical book expressing the views of this particular anti-Shakespearean sect is called *Francis the First: Unacknowledged King of Great Britain and Ireland.*[8] Since this Francis the First was also Shakespeare and Bacon and a score of other great writers, how can we mistake his titanic and mystical figure for anything but a culture hero? Apollo shrinks in comparison.

Adherents of Oxford, and members of other more recent sects, will disclaim such extremism and point to their own more modest claims. Still they are tending in the same direction. Proponents of Oxford are beginning to say that he was, if not the son, at least the paramour of Queen Elizabeth and the father of the earl of Southampton. Without wishing to misrepresent the views of individual anti-Stratfordians, which are quite various, the historian is bound to see the movement in the large and all of a piece. The initial step taken by every member of it, in repudiating the common man from Stratford, points to the destination at which the advance guard has already arrived, where one kneels at a mythical throne.

Our next consideration is the psychological basis of hero creation. Sigmund Freud and the depth psychologists have propounded a theory which has been given its classical expression by Otto Rank. In considering the phenomenon of similarity in the careers of culture heroes whenever and wherever they have appeared, the anthropologists used to debate whether the myths all stemmed from one central myth by some migratory process, or whether they originated independently and resembled each other because of some occult configuration of the primitive mind. Otto Rank finally pointed out that the really significant problem is why the central myth, if there was one, was the kind of thing it was, and why its features have proved so universally acceptable. His explanation is briefly as follows.

In a child's early consciousness, its father is a symbol of power, a king and god, but as the child grows aware of society beyond the hearth, the father shrinks in dimension. The man next door is bigger, the mayor of the town more respected, the lord of the manor more rich and grand. The child's original conception of his all-powerful father is surrendered as reluctantly as his original conception of his own central place in the universe. To recapture the original image, the child tends to substitute or adopt some more powerful person as father, one of the figures of wealth and power obtruded upon its eyes by the world at large. This rejection of the real father may look like treachery, but its basis is loyalty to the original mistaken conception. Veneration of the substitute father derives from an earlier veneration of the true father.

Many of us have forgotten such childhood reveries, but others will confess that we have had daydreams in which we figured as changelings, scions of the great, unjustly being reared in humble homes. Freud has given the term "family romance fantasy" to this species of reverie, and has demonstrated that its indulgence is normal unless, like other forms of immaturity, the indulgence persists. It can then, in extreme cases, become one of the symptoms of the hysteric or paranoiac; in fact it was through clinical findings that the prevalent nature of this type of reverie was discovered. When it does persist in significant measure, we speak in popular terms of megalomania, delusions of grandeur, and so on. In theory we all begin with a touch of it, since we all begin as one in the triad of child, nourishing mother, and protective all-powerful father. If we have more than a touch of it, then transferring the fantasy to another (Shakespeare, in the case

I am proposing) may prove a safety vent. This is Rank's explanation, and it seems a rational one, for the almost universal trait of double identity in culture heroes. Human beings are emotionally prepared by their own early sensations to accept it. We are born myth-believers, and some of us born mythmakers.

Following this idea through, we should expect a difference between those who passively approve of stories about people who are really different and greater in origin than they appear to be, and people who actively shape and promulgate these stories. The active anti-Shakespeareans should, in theory, be more touched by the "family romance fantasy" than the average, and more in need of some means of sublimating it. I have put this idea to the test, and have scrutinized the personalities of some of the more eminent anti-Shakespeareans: James Wilmot, the first on record; Delia Bacon, the most militant and pathetic; Mark Twain, the most fiery and artistic; and, finally, the most surprising, whose name I shall for the moment withhold.[9] Emerson does not belong among the mythmakers, although in 1845–1846 he expressed repugnance at the thought of the plays having been composed by a mere actor-entertainer. No more does Dickens, who in a letter to William Sandys on June 13, 1847, rejoiced that biographers had not succeeded in penetrating Shakespeare's privacy; he said, prophetically, "If he had had a Boswell, society wouldn't have respected his grave, but would calmly have had his skull in the phrenological shop windows." Dickens was active in the movement to preserve the Stratford birthplace, and is only one of a number of famous people who have, without reason, been claimed as adherents by the Baconians.

James Wilmot in the late eighteenth century communicated to a friend, James Cowell, his conviction that Shakespeare was Bacon. Cowell disclosed his friend's views in 1805 at a meeting of the Ipswich Philosophical Society, but the shocked members resolved not to mention the heresy abroad. Like many of his successors, Wilmot formulated his theory when he was an elderly man living in retirement. The son of an innkeeper and brother of a house painter, he lifted himself from his provincial environment to become a doctor of divinity and fellow of Oxford. But his success ended there, and the copious literary memorabilia of the Johnsonian era contain, so far as I can discover, no note of him. In his advancing years he seems to have drawn comfort from daydreams. We know of these only through the adulatory memoir of a niece whom he had reared, Olivia Wilmot Scrres. This, *The Life of the Author of the Letters of Junius, the Rev. James Wilmot, D.D.* (London, 1813), deserves attention as a literary curiosity. That Wilmot was himself largely responsible for his niece's conception of him is suggested by several factors. In some ways the volume is "scrupulous." Although it does not mention her uncle's Baconianism (still a secret at the time), it omits Shakespeare from the list of great authors whom Wilmot admired. On the other hand, Bacon figures quite prominently: her "venerated uncle greatly resembled Lord Bacon in person and mind" (p. 196). Numerous elements of the "family romance fantasy" appear, notably in the glorification of the Wilmot lineage (linked to that of the earls of Rochester), and in the conversion of the Wilmot inn into a "castle" maintained for the entertainment of guests as an eccentric hobby.

Perhaps the best indication that James Wilmot was himself responsible for Olivia's effusions as well as the Baconian theory is that her method of proving him (preposterously) the author of the *Letters of Junius* is the method by which he had proved Bacon the author of Shakespeare's plays. The method is that of inverted deduction—of fitting the head to the cap. Since Olivia was a notorious fraud, it is conceivable that she created her uncle's "career" out of whole cloth; however, it is difficult to imagine how she could have invented the eighteenth-century milieu without his aid. Enough of her material bears the mark of family transmission to suggest that the dim rector of Barlow-on-the-Heath was given to fantasies of personal grandeur.[10]

Wilmot was, we are told, known at Oxford as "popularity Wilmot" and "Jemmy Wise" or "Jemmy Right." A bishop's miter had often been dangled before him, but he had preserved his integrity by stalwartly refusing it. He was the intimate friend and valued correspondent of the peerage and royal family. His friend Hogarth had found his features too animated to be drawn. His sallies of wit had forced Garrick and other members of the smart set to slink from public places in chagrin. He secretly guided the statecraft of the king's ministers, but gave counsel also to their opponent Edmund Burke. Dr. Johnson submitted his writings to Wilmot for approval before venturing to publish them. He guided Johnson's studies at Oxford, and tried to befriend him by buying him shoes. Since Johnson left Oxford when Wilmot was only three years old, this was one of his more difficult feats; however, it could have been Olivia's own flourish. To her I would certainly attribute the claim that Wilmot had performed several secret marriages for George III and had himself secretly married the princess of Poland. But even these stories may have had their origin in dark hints from the subject himself. The pioneer Baconian seems pretty clearly to have been a victim of mild megalomania, living in his own special world of myths.

The case of Delia Bacon is too clear-cut to require much comment.[11] In some ways she was a heroic and admirable woman. Born in poverty and self-educated, she became a public lecturer on cultural subjects, a living symbol of woman's right to an intellectual life. Possessed of such an active mind and such demonic energy as almost to succeed in shaping herself into the grandiose self-image she nourished, she was nevertheless that most dangerous of all people to know, the plausible fantast, and she left a trail of human damage—to one young clergyman harassed for alleged breach of promise and to many friends and relatives forced to lick their wounds and count their financial losses. Her kindest benefactor, Nathaniel Hawthorne, cried at last in despair, "I will never be kind to anybody again as long as I live." He continued to be kind to Delia, and has been rewarded by being erroneously listed as a Baconian in the manuals. In the period just before she exploded her anti-Shakespearean bomb in 1857, those closest to Delia Bacon knew that she was walking the thin edge. Her brother was certain she would go completely mad if allowed to indulge her monomania, while Hawthorne was hopeful that the indulgence might save her. Both were mistaking the symptoms for the disease. She died an institutionalized paranoiac, showing symptoms of the "family romance fantasy." Though presumably aware, as an "expert," that Bacon had left no issue, she claimed descent from him in conversation with an authentic woman intellectual, Maria Mitchell, the American astronomer.[12]

So far as Mark Twain is concerned, a whole essay could be written on his hate-affair with Shakespeare, who became in his emotional life a *bête noire* rivaling even Mary Baker Eddy. In his last book, *Is Shakespeare Dead?* Mark Twain avers that he always suspected that the man from Stratford had not written the plays, and that he is now sure of it.[13] The book was issued as an installment of his autobiography and is extremely personal. Amidst its heavy sarcasms at the expense of Shakespeare and his superstitious admirers runs a plaintive vein of boasting, about Mark Twain's own past glories as a pilot, his disregarded wisdom, his great reputation in his native Hannibal compared with Shakespeare's small reputation in his native Stratford, and the like. Some of the reviewers thought this must be intended as humor, but it was not. The book is one of the saddest ever written. Van Wyck

Brooks, writing in 1920, attributes this book and Mark Twain's ever-increasing morbidity to a guilt complex, induced by the fact that he had never realized himself as an artist; but I suspect that this is because Brooks himself would have preferred him to become some other kind of artist than he actually became. Most of us have no quarrel with Mark Twain as an artist. Although the diagnosis of Brooks strikes me as wrong, his observations of the symptoms are acute. He asks why the "subject of dual personality was always . . . an obsession with Mark Twain," why he was always preoccupied with "the theme of the lost heir and usurper? why is it that the idea of changelings in the cradle perpetually haunted his mind?"[14] Brooks was evidently unaware that modern psychology has classified such fixations and given them a clinical label.

Mark Twain himself speaks of his own "cloudy sense . . . of having been a prince, once, in some enchanted far-off land, & of being in exile now, & desolate—& lord, no chance to ever get back there again!"[15] He viewed his *Adventures of Tom Sawyer* as "simply a hymn put into prose." A hymn to what? It is startling to reread this book after reading Otto Rank and others who have analyzed the nature of childhood reveries of grandeur. All of us realize that Tom is Mark himself, and Sid is Mark's actual brother, and that the heavenly St. Petersburg is Hannibal, Missouri. But though the book is packed with the spirit of domesticity, where are Tom's father and mother? The mother is transformed into the virginal Aunt Polly, and the father is completely expunged. The father finally "adopted" by Tom is the most eminent man of the town, Judge Thatcher. Tom is inescapably the mythical superchild, triumphing in every conceivable role. He enjoys not one resurrection but two. In the first of these, he triumphantly heads the procession of three boys walking down a church aisle to attend their own funeral, while the congregation bursts out in a historic rendering of "Praise

God from Whom All Blessings Flow." To remember how one rejoiced in this dream-book as a boy is to feel a little abashed. For the author himself to have rejoiced in it, instead of in his true masterpiece, *Huckleberry Finn,* is surely suggestive.

Another of Mark Twain's own favorites among his works was *The Prince and the Pauper,* in which the hapless Prince Edward suffers harrowing adventures as a waif of the London slums, while a beggar boy occupies the throne that is rightfully his. General readers will probably be most familiar with this favorite theme in *Pudd'nhead Wilson,* in which the white Tom Driscoll is reared among Negroes, while the white Negro, Valet de Chambre, exchanged for him in the cradle, usurps his place in an aristocratic home. Mark Twain's waifs are conceived with an emotional consistency which distinguishes them from other fictional waifs of the time—those of Charles Dickens, for instance. Dickens' waifs do not turn out to be princes and transplanted aristocrats. Although psychological probings are quite irrelevant in the critical evaluation of the artist's work, the fact remains that these changelings of Mark Twain are probably a sublimation of his own "cloudy sense of having been a prince," and that those intimates who playfully addressed him as Messiah and King knew how to please. In some ways he seems the very epitome of the man who is a man for a' that, and *Huckleberry Finn* itself is a hymn to democratic decency; and yet this author is the one who craved, as he said, to wear a "flowing costume made all of silks and velvets resplendent with shining dyes," but who settled for a suit of apostolic white. He never claimed that he, the boy from Hannibal, was really a king or messiah. Instead he claimed that Shakespeare, the boy from Stratford, was really a lord. And yet he professed to despise lords. I am not claiming that the "character" of this genius presents a simple problem.

If the present discussion has taken a somewhat Freudian

turn, the fact should not be surprising when we identify the fourth prominent anti-Shakespearean, who seems to sub-stantiate the theory that the more militant members of the sect are apt to be people in whom the "family romance fantasy" persists beyond childhood. This fourth example is none other than Sigmund Freud himself. Freud was obsessed by the Shakespearean controversy throughout his life. His own three heroes, the ones with whom he tended to identify, were Moses, Leonardo da Vinci, and Shakespeare; and he felt that there was some mystery about the identity of all of them. He decided finally that Moses was not really a Levite but a noble Egyptian, even though Freud himself was Jewish and loyal to his race if not its religion. For a time he was attracted to the theory that Shakespeare was really French, his name de-riving from "Jacques" and "Pierre." This is completely typical Baconian reasoning. In 1922 he read a book ad-vancing the claims of the earl of Oxford as author of Shake-speare's plays, and he finally became an ardent convert to this faith.[16] The fact that he had formerly related the Oedipus complex of Hamlet to the death of Shakespeare's father in 1601 did not deter him. With his usual fortitude, he proceeded to transfer the biographical speculations he had printed about *Hamlet* and *Lear* to the life of the earl of Oxford.[17] Against the advice of his editors and friends, he stubbornly proclaimed his new faith, in public speeches and in a revision of his autobiography. As he grew older, he grew more and more aggressive in his anti-Shakespeareanism, and called the English persistence in believing in Shakespeare a "narcissistic defense." This is a new language of religious controversy. Mark Twain's words for belief in Shakespeare had been "bigotry," "superstition," and "fetishism," compar-able to belief in witches, Satan, and infant damnation.

Now Freud, we must recall, is the one who identified the "family romance fantasy" in which the fantast's "parents are replaced by others of better birth."[18] Could it possibly be that Freud himself was of the type in which the residue of this fantasy persists to an abnormal degree? The analysis of analysts had best be left to fellow analysts—in the present instance to Freud's own greatest disciple, admirer, and biographer, Ernest Jones. This is what Jones says about Freud's anti-Shakespeareanism:

I am suggesting that something in Freud's mentality led him to take a special interest in people not being what they seemed to be . . . the Oxford idea must have come as a relief. He told Eitingon that there were two themes that "always perplexed him to distraction": the Bacon-Shakespeare controversy and the question of telepathy. . . . From all this discussion about identity it may well be surmised that we are concerned with some derivative of the Family Romance phantasy in Freud. He had indeed mentioned himself a rather similar conscious phantasy from his youth: the wish that he had been Emmanuel's son and thus had an easier path in life. What is interesting, however, is not that Freud's personality should have contained similar elements to those of lesser mortals, but that they should have been able to disturb his mind in such a remote fashion.[19]

On this testimony, in traditional phrasing, the case rests. James Wilmot, Delia Bacon, Mark Twain, Sigmund Freud— the eccentric recluse, the woman possessed, the literary genius, and the pioneer of the human subconscious—again we see what Coleridge speaks of as "unity in multeity" in the operation of the human mind, and also that thin line which often separates mental distinction and aberration. There has been no intention in the present essay to attack the anti-Shakespearean movement by discrediting witnesses. In matters of literary history, these four possess no authority that needs discrediting. The intention has been, not to attack them but to explain them, and through them a certain type of mythmaking, and through mythmaking the "authorship controversy." Both Freud and Mark Twain were great and good men. Dubious as his influence sometimes seems to be, it would be hard to find in the annals of human endeavor a greater devotion than Freud's to what he thought of as human service. And in the annals of human relations, it would be hard to find more loyalty and kindness than Mark Twain's toward his blood relations. Oddly enough, all four of these persons, however prone to the "family romance fantasy," were very loyal to their real families on the practical level. Such is the complexity of the human individual. It should not surprise us too much to find a subconscious predisposition to mythmaking in Mark Twain and Freud; the first, after all, is the great mythmaker of America, and the second, with Marx, one of the two great mythmakers of the modern world.

The attacks upon Shakespeare's authorship, then, must be referred, not to the realm of biographical and literary evidence, but to the realm of mythmaking. And mythmaking has its permanent bastion in the twilight zone of the human mind. The impulse accounting for these attacks is the same basic impulse which accounts for the creation of our Siegfrieds and our King Arthurs, and perhaps the proper attitude toward them is not angry indignation but wonder. It is not the least of Shakespeare's distinctions that he has been singled out to become the one culture hero of modern times, the single addition to ancient pantheons. True, since it has arisen in the period of documented facts and a scientific regard for evidence, the idea that the author of *Hamlet* and *Lear* was a kingly-godly figure from whom all the wisdom of the Renaissance emanated is what might be called an "inhibited" myth. But this is only Shakespeare's quadricentenary. Who knows what idea may prevail at his millenary?

As we speculate about the nature of any man, it is relevant, I believe, to consider the kind of man he admires and would presumably wish to be like. It is at least as logical to identify the "real" man with his aspirations as with his id. The following essay was written with no thought of biographical probing, but it may have some bearing upon the subject of Shakespeare's personality.

ADMIRERS of Shakespeare are apt to smile a little at Schiller's *Don Carlos,* with its manifest defects as theatrical art, but few can remain untouched by its fervor: the moral excitement of its youthful composer still glows in every line. It was written slightly past midway between Shakespeare's time and our own, and it was once hailed as giving to drama the one thing that Shakespeare had withheld. What this thing is, is best illustrated in the character of the Marquis de Posa, a Spanish grandee who, in lonely righteousness, opposes the terrible Philip, the bloody Alva, and the baleful figure of the Grand Inquisitor. Although de Posa's immediate mission is to save the threatened burghers of Flanders, his martyrdom is for all mankind. He is presented as Christlike, as a symbol of moral beauty, as a citizen of a future world of freedom, equality, and loving-kindness. So generous is the impulse that inspired his creation that we dare not use his own words cynically against him— that those who would serve their fellow men must somewhat resemble them.

Shakespeare gives us no character like the Marquis de Posa. Perhaps, if he had done so, Emerson would have called him the "poet priest." Emerson denied Shakespeare this accolade in his *Representative Men* in 1850. In 1861, another great liberal, Giuseppe Mazzini, prefaced a collection of his critical writings with the avowal of his own belief that "art is a moral priesthood."[1] For Mazzini, Schiller qualified as the poet priest by representing in such a character as the Marquis de Posa "the principle of right, of freedom of thought, of progress, the soul of the universe."[2] Mazzini would give Schiller to Italian youth to read entire. The only other dramatists he would give entire to the rising generation were Aeschylus and Shakespeare, both selected because they *paved the way* for Schiller. Shakespeare, although magnificent, was in the last analysis only the poet of the Middle Ages, the poet of the individual. His characters are "not symbols of any absolute or ideal type" and convey "no universal law acting upon collective humanity; no social religious idea."[3]

There are interesting parallels between the thought of Mazzini and of a later philosopher-critic of Latin lineage, George Santayana. The latter notes "the absence of religion" in Shakespeare, his lack of allegiance to any ideal or system, and wonders if perhaps "the northern mind, even in him, did not remain morose and barbarous in its inmost core."[4] Mazzini had spoken of "those reflections on the nullity of human things and the worthlessness of life which so constantly recur throughout his plays" with their distressing effect upon the "youthful soul."[5] Both critics quote Macbeth's "Tomorrow, and tomorrow, and tomorrow," but Santayana is the more incautious of the two in accepting it as Shakespeare's ultimate philosophy. Mazzini believes that Shakespeare teaches us "calmly to face and despise both life and death."[6] These particular words were written in 1830 and thus anticipate T. S. Eliot's[7] by about a century in "proposing" a stoical Shakespeare. Mazzini is not scornful of stoicism in the fashion of Eliot, but he views it certainly as only second best. Shakespeare's characters, who accept the universe, will do well enough until Schiller's appear: these will gloriously transform it.

Schiller and Mazzini have not occupied our minds very much of late, and it may seem invidious to pair their names. A voice from Germany spoke and a voice from Italy responded. That later voices from Germany and responses from Italy were so different should not tempt us to say that Shakespeare represents the more temperate spirit of an Anglo-American axis, avoiding ideological extremes and consequent disaster in the practical world. The distinction between Shakespeare and Schiller is not a national one, and dissatisfaction with Shakespeare's ideals or lack of them has not been confined to foreign lands. "Caesar was not in Shakespeare," says Bernard Shaw, craving a symbol-Caesar of triumphant practicality.[8] Frank Harris, most incongruously, maintained that Christ and Mahomet were not in him. Walt Whitman at least implied that Abraham Lincoln was not in him—and thus it goes. To whatever extent we remain unconvinced that Shakespeare's spiritual capacity was less than that of those who bring the charges, we must recognize the fact that no Lincoln, Christ, or symbol-Caesar of triumphant practicality appears in his dramatis personae. A critic like Dowden moderately concedes the deficiency: "We need to supplement the noble positivism of Shakespeare."[9] He instances such poets as Wordsworth, Shelley, Newman, and Whitman as providing that supplement. The point is precisely the same. Since Shakespeare was a dramatist, the only way he himself could have provided the supplement would have been to create characters like the Marquis de Posa—symbolizing freedom, holiness, brotherhood, social justice, or whatever the ideals might be, Wordsworthian, Whitmanesque, or Shavian, individually endorsed or universally yearned after.

The usual defense of Shakespeare is that his characters symbolize no great ideals because they represent actual men with all their merits and defects. Schiller's Marquis de Posa is a group of ideas, whereas Shakespeare's Brutus is a man. The defense is persuasive, but is based upon a fallacy. Shakespeare's Brutus is *not* a man. He is not even a portrait of a man, except in the limited sense in which all characterization may be called portraiture. Brutus is the literary projection of Shakespeare's *conception* of a man. He is a character in a play, consisting of a number of traits synthesized in his creator's imagination, and is therefore as much a group of ideas as is the Marquis de Posa. We must not be evasive. If the Marquis de Posa had appeared in a play by Shakespeare, he could have retained his program and voiced his high aspirations without seeming any less a man than Brutus. Shakespeare's characters seem lifelike because of Shakespeare's technique. We may go so far as to say that his technique is his most distinguishing quality, and that he was more concerned with the plausibility and interest of his characters than with the value of the ideas they represent, but we must not say that his characters are not characters. When we say that the Marquis de Posa is a group of ideas, we are saying what is true; our words are reliable because Schiller's play has not succeeded in "taking us in." When we say that Brutus is a man, our words are unreliable because Shakespeare's play *has* succeeded in "taking us in."

Brutus and the Marquis de Posa are no different generically. Each came out of a dramatist's head. Each is a symbol. To say that Shakespeare does not symbolize ideals is to mistake the nature of art, and to recognize no distinction between how skillfully an artist does a thing and what it is that he does. It assumes that symbols that are lifelike are no longer symbols. An artist deals in symbols and in nothing else. Falstaff is as much a symbol as Brutus or the Marquis de Posa, but he symbolizes a different thing. Shakespeare's "good" characters are composites of qualities mainly good, given a local habitation and a name, a deceptive appearance of reality. Henry the Fifth is a symbol of something that Shakespeare and those who gave him a favorable hearing conceived to be very good, just as the Marquis de Posa is a symbol of something that Schiller and those who gave *him* a favorable hearing conceived to be very good. That Henry the Fifth is able to unbend and play practical jokes, as the Marquis de Posa is not, and thus has for us a greater appearance of reality and a greater human interest, does not alter the fact that Henry wants to acquire France and de Posa wants to free Flanders. It does not refute the assertion that a character who wants to free Flanders symbolizes a higher ideal than does one who wants to acquire France.

Shakespeare's characters are symbols, and his good characters symbolize ideals conceived by Shakespeare to be good. Before we decide the extent to which these ideals are deficient, we ought to decide what they are. There are many ways in which the inquiry might proceed. The one chosen in the present essay is intended to eliminate such things as Henry the Fifth's humorous whimsies so that we will not be diverted by Shakespeare's artistic cunning. Those shrewd touches of nature, those living lineaments, those fascinating notes of reserve which make us forget that Shakespeare's symbols are, after all, symbols only, will be blanked out. We will deal with abstract qualities alone, in the hope of discovering the pattern adumbrated by all of Shakespeare's admirable men—the pattern from which the Marquis de Posa presumably departs.

The reader will recollect many speeches, like Antony's tribute to Brutus at one extreme and Polonius' prudential maxims to Laertes at the other, in which ideals of character are expressed. In the tribute to Brutus [10] unselfishness and equanimity are the dominant qualities suggested. In a corresponding tribute to Hamlet, the qualities are regal and soldierly—"For he was likely . . ." [11] Helena's stated reasons

for loving Bertram are simply, "His archèd brows, his hawking eye, his curls."[12] The quality stressed may be tolerance
as in the case of the elder Bertram,[13] or self-control as in the
case of Horatio.[14] Usually a number of qualities are included
in a single speech. Ophelia speaks of Hamlet's "noble mind"
and his

> ... tongue, sword,
> The courtier's, scholar's, soldier's eye,
> Th' expectancy and rose of the fair state,
> The glass of fashion and the mould of form . . .[15]

Capulet describes his candidate for Juliet's hand as

> A gentleman of noble parentage,
> Of fair demesnes, youthful, and nobly trained,
> Stuffed, as they say, with honorable parts,
> Proportioned as one's thoughts would wish a man.[16]

A young woman is apt to list the same qualities but place the
emphasis a little differently. Olivia speaks of Orsino:

> ... I suppose him virtuous, know him noble,
> Of great estate, of fresh and stainless youth;
> In voices well divulged, free, learned and valiant,
> And in dimension and the shape of nature
> A gracious person.[17]

Sometimes the application is quite general:

... do you know what a man is? Is not birth, beauty, good shape,
discourse, manhood, learning, gentleness, virtue, youth, liberality
and such like, the spice and salt that season a man?[18]

Sometimes the ideal is presented negatively, as when Proteus
proposes to slander Valentine "with falsehood, cowardice,
and poor descent,"[19] or when Viola cries,

> I hate ingratitude more in a man
> Than lying, vainness, babbling, drunkenness
> Or any taint of vice whose strong corruption
> Inhabits our frail blood.[20]

The shorter the speech, the more apt it is to include indispensables, like Portia's terse characterization of Bassanio as "a scholar and a soldier," [21] or the Duke of Vienna's defense of himself as "a scholar, a statesman, and a soldier." [22] The prominence of courage and brains among the valued traits receives emphasis from the fact that the despicable ones, Thurio, Slender, Sir Andrew Aguecheek, and the like, are nearly always both cowardly and silly.

If we examine the many speeches [23] in which the merits or defects of men are inventoried, we will find every conceivable quality listed, but some so frequently repeated, by so many different types of speaker in so many different circumstances, as to achieve the status of universal application. These indispensable qualities are three in number, and are most commonly designated by terms that seem now somewhat quaint. The right kind of man must be *scholarly, soldierly,* and *honest*. It is well that he be also handsome, well-born, opulent, generous, kind, and even possess the social graces. It is well that he be open-minded, or "free," as Olivia tells Malvolio. But he *must be* scholarly, soldierly, and honest. Good men may deviate from this norm; their minds may be abused or their honesty disordered by their passions; but only the fools and villains are incurable.

By *scholarly* Shakespeare means intelligent and well informed, educated, *schooled,* whether formally or by natural aptitude sharpened by experience of the world. A few of his heroes such as Dukes Vincentio and Prospero have a record of retreat into their libraries, but a trace of guilt attaches itself to it. Ordinarily the characters praised as scholarly are not "bookish" or specialized in their interests. Hamlet may suggest to us the studious and contemplative man, but Bassanio and Orsino do not; yet Bassanio is a "scholar" and Orsino is "learned." Shakespeare would not have called a scholar *scholarly* if the process of specialization had dwarfed his general interests. The dramatist's high regard for the active and informed mind goes far to explain his alleged contempt for the lower classes. When artisans attempt to govern the state, perform plays, or debate philosophy, he is not socially incensed but he is certainly amused—they simply do not *know* enough.

By *soldierly* Shakespeare means courageous and strong, capable of effective physical action. Hamlet may be out of training and may have little experience in the field, but he is soldierly nevertheless—worthy to be borne from the stage by four captains. He can, on occasion, prove a tall man of his hands, an able swordsman, and could, if necessary, submit to discipline, master tactics, and lead men. No superlative endowment of wisdom, talent, or virtue whatsoever excuses a man from being capable in combat. A saint who is not soldierly can aspire to no higher role than that of Henry the Sixth. The right kind of man must be willing to sell his life, and able to sell it dear. The single claim to exemption is old age, and one of the most curious and sometimes distressing details of the Shakespearean attitude is revealed when his aged men, who have retained their courage but lost the strength to implement it, are portrayed as futile and ridiculous.

By *honest,* Shakespeare means reliable, moral, virtuous—everything that implies deference to the conventional code of right conduct prevalent in the character's circle. The word in his time had not the almost exclusive connotation of respect for property rights that it has since, significantly, acquired. In Shakespeare, it is as dishonest to make love to a man's wife as to pick his pocket or cheat him at cards; it is as dishonest for a sentry to sleep at his post as to sell secrets to the enemy. There is nothing experimental, exploratory, or critical in the concept. Honesty is doing what is generally recognized to be *right*. In the last analysis it is the quality that makes a man act for the common good, with the nature of such action determined not by the man himself but by the accumulated experience of his race and expressed in simple and clearly defined rules. The order of precedence of the rules is itself predetermined. Ingratitude is always dishonest. Lying may or may not be, according to the circumstances.

There is no inevitable occurrence in the inventories of words signifying that a man should be pious; in fact such words rarely occur at all. That he should not be actively irreligious, or atheistical, is implied by the comprehensive term *honest,* but Shakespeare's pagans are as honest as his Christians, and both classes are presented with equally few particulars about their piety. That his characters are not delineated as devout, that religion appears as a well-spring of action in few of them, has been noted and deplored. The phenomenon should not be discussed in isolation. His characters are with equal rarity praised for being humanitarian, truthful, or just. There is no insistence upon qualities more imposing than those of immediate use in the character's immediate world. That we are not dealing merely with words, and with their chance occurrence and nonoccurrence, may be demonstrated by the way in which one of the more abstract virtues fares in the action. Shakespeare's good characters are not praised for being truthful, and for very good reason—truthful they rarely are.

Hamlet thus excuses the wrong he has done Laertes:

> Give me your pardon, sir. I have done you wrong,
> But pardon't, as you are a gentleman.
> This presence knows, and you must needs have heard
> How I am punished with sore distraction.
> What I have done
> That might your nature, honor, and exception
> Roughly awake, I here proclaim was madness.
> Was't Hamlet that wronged Laertes? Never Hamlet.

If Hamlet from himself be ta'en away,
And when he's not himself does wrong Laertes,
Then Hamlet it is not, Hamlet denies it.
Who does it then? His madness.[24]

Since Hamlet is not truly mad, this speech is a circumstantial lie, and as such it offended Dr. Johnson.[25] Kittredge defends Hamlet thus:

"I wish Hamlet had made some other defence; it is unsuitable to the character of a good or a brave man to shelter himself in falsehood" (Johnson). It is odd that Dr. Johnson failed to see that Hamlet's particular falsehood here is inseparable from the general falsehood involved in his counterfeiting madness. If his conduct here is to be reprehended, the blame should go farther back and attach itself to his whole stratagem, and no one has ever taken ethical ground against that.[26]

But Hamlet also lies without reference to his stratagem:

Rosencrantz. My lord, you once did love me.
Hamlet. And do still, by these pickers and stealers.[27]

Coleridge and Strachey took pains to explain away this deviation also,[28] but the fact remains that Hamlet's standards are not strict. Although it is quite true that his lie to Laertes is related to his stratagem, it is not told in order to advance that stratagem; rather, a past event is used as a convenience to ease a present situation, and the speech qualifies as a lie no matter how irreprehensible. And although no ethical ground has been taken against the stratagem itself, the fact remains that it might be. Readers of the play have simply concurred in the assumption that deceit may be practiced in a worthy cause, that ends justify means—including falsehood of both word and action. One suspects that the classical view that comedy should deal with base characters is linked with the fact that comedy, not tragedy, is usually concerned with stratagems.

Practically all of Shakespeare's characters lie, even the best of them, and the women as frequently as the men. When the good Duke Humphrey is arranging a duel and is asked by his king what he is saying, he replies "Talking of hawking; nothing else, my lord." [29] When the sheriff asks for Falstaff, who is behind the curtain, Prince Hal says, "The man, I do assure you, is not here ..."; [30] and he shows no more devotion to the truth after his reform and ascent of the throne. [31] Portia, although she elsewhere expresses her aversion for him, assures the Prince of Morocco that if her choice were free,

> Yourself, renownèd Prince, then stood as fair
> As any comer I have looked on yet
> For my affection. [32]

Paulina affirms vehemently that Hermione is dead, deceiving the audience as well as the other characters in the play.

> I say she's dead; I'll swear't. If word nor oath
> Prevail not, go and see. [33]

Antony's bare-faced lie to Octavia [34] does not impugn his standing as a man of honor, nor Florizel's detailed lie to Leontes [35] his standing as a fresh and chivalrous youth. Young women in love, otherwise so clear and stainless, show a masterful duplicity, Helena, [36] Olivia, [37] Portia, [38] and the rest; Juliet is one of the most accomplished liars in literature. [39] The innocent maidens are matched in this department only by the holy friars—Laurence, [40] Francis, [41] and Peter. [42] Even when the lie has debatable motives or evil consequences, like Ophelia's, [43] or Emilia's, [44] or Volumnia's, [45] the teller is indicted in our minds not for falsehood but for weakness or poor judgment. A few of the lies are glorious, like Desdemona's exoneration of Othello, [46] but the great majority of them are designed to further a ruse, ease an awkward moment, or serve as a minor convenience.

Brutus is the most finical of Shakespeare's men. "Swear

priests and cowards and men cautelous," he cries when an oath is proposed among the conspirators. He wants no other oath "than honesty to honesty engaged." [47] There is pride in the speech, an insistence that Brutus's word is as good as his bond, but there is also a notion of transcendental virtue. As a rule the characters welcome vows. Ceremonial is concrete, and for a moment the great abstractions become semivisible. When Imogen gives a false name, she says to herself,

> If I do lie and do
> No harm by it, though the gods hear, I hope
> They'll pardon it.[48]

Her self-consciousness in the matter is most untypical of Shakespeare. Lying in these plays conveys no sense of guilt, and is thus distinguished from lying, even "white" lying, on the part of good characters in, let us say, the nineteenth-century novel. The reason has already been indicated. The indispensable virtues of men as deduced from the inventories, and exemplified by the actions of the admirable characters in the plays as a whole, fail to imply devotion to truthfulness. The truth as an abstraction commands no loyalty in the Shakespearean world.

The Shakespearean man is not required to act upon a nice consideration of abstract principle in general. He feels no compulsion to relieve wants other than those about him, or to right wrongs other than those he sees. A good man's ministry is to particular men and not to mankind. The most striking statement of the superior claim of justice over mercy is voiced by Angelo:

> *Isabella.*   Yet show some pity.
> *Angelo.* I show it most of all when I show justice,
>   For then I pity those I do not know . . .[49]

But this play, like all the other plays, comes nearer to vindicating compromise than absolute justice. The characters in general want mercy for themselves and their friends, and justice for their enemies and strangers; or, putting it less stridently, justice appears to them more venerable than mercy but not nearly so pleasant. Angelo's devotion to exemplary justice comes near to being portrayed, even before his fall from grace, as an eccentricity and defect of character. Even in Shakespeare's good men, devotion to the more transcendental virtues is apt to appear as disabling. Hamlet yearns for the absolute, but Hamlet is fatally confused. Brutus has a passion for purity in leadership, but Brutus leads men to their doom. In Shakespeare, the expression of our finest aspirations is often put into the mouths of the defective or the despised. John Ball cries for social justice, but John Ball is fiercely predatory. Henry the Sixth cries for peace and forbearance, but Henry the Sixth is pusillanimous. Shylock pleads the case of our common humanity, but Shylock is an embittered outcast.

In view of the chillingly finite nature of Shakespearean ideals as thus far described, what can be said in his defense? Nothing? a little? or everything? The answer is *almost* everything. We should notice, first of all, that his soldierly, scholarly, honest man, while completely acceptable in his milieu, is not completely acceptable to himself. He is not smug, self-righteous, convinced of his own perfection. There hovers about him a consciousness of his own inadequacy, a latent sense of guilt.

Polonius. My lord, I will use them according to their desert.
Hamlet. God's bodykins, man, much better! Use every man after his desert, and who should scape whipping?[50]

We should notice, also, that the appeals for social justice, human equality, and the like do not receive summary condemnation along with those who utter them. Even Angelo is not successfully argued down; it is he and his apostasy that are condemned rather than his program of reform. The portraits of John Ball and Shylock represent less a rejection of progressive principles than a recognition of historical fact: great aspirations are born of great needs; cries for inclusion come from the excluded; shares are not given but demanded and then wrested away. Dealing with the somewhat intangible, we should notice that although there is no all-pervasive love of distant peoples enjoined in Shakespeare, there is also no all-pervasive hatred. Unconsciously, at least, he is something of an internationalist. Unless they are actively at war with his nation, he pays foreigners the high compliment of thinking of them as English. The French were reputedly arrogant, but Shakespeare's most democratic king is French.[51] The Russians were reputedly bizarre and barbaric, but Russian Hermione is most gently civilized. Italy was reputedly the land of lust, but most of Shakespeare's pure lovers are Italian. With him, the difference among the races of the world seemed only skin-deep: Othello is a Moor as well as Aaron, Jessica Jewish as well as Shylock. One other word, in this somewhat scattered phase of the defense: the absence of devotion to the more elevated principles seems little handicap to the characters in filling the roles most available to them. Although poorly equipped to be pacifists, emancipators, or humanitarians, they make good kings, subjects, masters, servants, fathers, sons, husbands, and lovers. One is optimistic if one dismisses this much as a trifle, or relegates these characters to an ethical wilderness.

The best vindication of Shakespeare's ideal man is supplied, not by the fugitive impressions mentioned thus far, but by the capacity for growth resident in one of his three cardinal qualities. The ideal man is *scholarly*. At the moment we meet him, he is simply not scholarly enough. What strikes us most forcibly about him in his function as a power for good is his limited imagination. Antonio is a scholarly, soldierly, honest man, but his scholarship fails to embrace an adequate knowledge of Jewish history or of the psychological effects of persecution upon racial and religious minorities. If he were as well informed as we are upon these matters, he could not have spat upon Shylock's gaberdine. His honesty would have forbade it. If others had attempted to do so, his courage would have prevented it. We remember Lear's words in his moment of vision.

> O, I have ta'en
> Too little care of this! Take physic, pomp;
> Expose thyself to feel what wretches feel,
> That thou mayst shake the superflux to them
> And show the heavens more just.[52]

Shakespeare's characters in general have *ta'en too little care*. They have failed to collect the necessary data and to engage in the necessary reflection to keep their system of collective welfare adequately revised. There is some excuse for them in that they live in a less complex society than ours and feel that they can accomplish much by doing the good closest at hand. Their deficiency is a practical one. The only true charge that can be lodged against them is that they lack the ideas that will solve the problems that we wish solved. The Marquis de Posa is not a better man than Henry the Fifth. He has merely, we presume, a better program.

The intention of these remarks is not to defend Shakespeare on an historical basis—on the ground that his ideal man is as virtuous as his age would tolerate. The intention is to point out that the distinction between Shakespeare's ideal man and Schiller's Marquis de Posa is not one of virtue at all. A subject of Henry the Fifth, so solicitous for the welfare of the peasants of Picardy as to oppose the invasion of France, would have seemed to Shakespeare *morally* offensive. The King himself is as solicitous for the welfare of these peasants as propriety will allow; they are not to be pillaged and are to receive, when the conquest is over, the inestimable boon of rule by England. To Shakespeare the Marquis de Posa, intriguing against his own nation on behalf of Flanders, would have seemed an eccentric, comic, or useless fellow, if not a downright villain. The loss of faith in existing institutions, one's own church and state and their duly authorized heads, as the best available means of achieving collective welfare is an intellectual phenomenon. It is the *idea* of revolution. It appears in Schiller, but does not appear in Shakespeare; there is no more to it than that. We must quote Mazzini once more: "in Shakespeare the *Ego* reached its highest formula, unaccompanied by any synthetical conception or love of the collective, yet preparing the way for both by a sublime affirmation of individual power and individual right." [53] Inevitably, the first part of this statement conveys the impression that the store of righteousness of Shakespeare's good men is too small to extend out far beyond themselves. Such is not the case. In them the "synthetical conception or love of the collective" exists, but takes the form of trust in and fidelity to the inherited institutions and the recognized leaders. As human knowledge has grown, the inadequacy of certain received institutions and their human pillars has become increasingly manifest—manifest to scholarly men like Shakespeare's.

If Schiller has progressed beyond Shakespeare or if we have progressed beyond either, it is on the intellectual plane, and it is absurd to bring charges of spiritual deficiency. The Marquis de Posa is a martyr. Those who assert that Shakespeare has given us no martyrs are most unobservant. What they really mean is that he has given us no martyrs for *their* causes. He has given us many martyrs, for king and country, for factions—above all, for beloved individuals. The great thing is that martyrdom itself is not alien to them. They will die for what is right as the right appears to them. There is as much moral fervor in these characters as the world can possibly use. All soldierly, scholarly, honest men are potential martyrs; they need only a proper occasion.

We admire the Marquis de Posa but must recognize that, in the last analysis, he is worth no more than the practicality of his plan. It is difficult to see how one system for implementing the "synthetical conception or love of the collective" can be valued above another except on the basis of its utility. There is value, of course, in experimentation, but experimentation seems often to bring with it a sense of suspended responsibility. In brooding over panaceas, we neglect to administer homely remedies; in regarding ourselves as citizens of the future, we neglect our duties in the present. Even in the Marquis de Posa himself, and in ourselves as we read Schiller's play, we are sometimes uneasily aware of a basking in the *emotion* of benevolence, detached from its practical effects. Perhaps this is the great malady of the modern age. One thing that sends us back to Shakespeare for strength and refreshment is that his good people are incorrupt. They do not luxuriate in impulses of goodness, but act upon them within their limited sphere. The emphasis is upon achievement. The beneficiaries are never, as in Schiller, completely out of sight. We have the impression that as the knowledge of Shakespeare's characters grows, their courage and honesty will keep pace. If our own courage and honesty had kept pace with our knowledge, we would now be living in Utopia. We show a defect from which Shakespeare was free; we revere high ideals simply as high ideals, and tend to respond to them sentimentally. We take pleasure, as Shakespeare refused to do, simply in *righteous sensations*.

Shakespeare's ideal woman had also three indispensable qualities. To correspond to his soldierly, scholarly, honest man, his ideal woman had to be gentle, chaste, and fair. These requirements are not such low ones after all. In

Restoration times they seemed rather high. Thomas Otway's voice is nostalgic:

> My father was (a thing now rare)
> Loyal and brave, my mother chaste and fair.[54]

The famous lines of Otway's great contemporary filter away the intangibles altogether:

> Happy, happy, happy pair!
>   None but the brave,
>   None but the brave,
>   None but the brave deserves the fair.[55]

The ideal expressed in these lines is purely aristocratic. Shakespeare's ideal man borrows virtue from the aristocracy, of course, but from other social strata as well: this man possesses middle-class honesty and even a clerkly regard for the well-furnished and active mind.

*I*N A RECENT issue of the *Shakespeare Newsletter* the ever-helpful editor listed thirty-four things which might be done at a quadricentenary celebration. Of only one of these would I disapprove—the holding of a debate on the authorship question. Picture us sheepishly dispersing if the wrong side won, filled with delicacies which should rightfully have been consumed on some other date! The mode of celebration selected by The Shakespeare Association of America is less risky for the celebrants generally, and has its roots in deep antiquity. A feast is held and someone is designated, on this great anniversary of this great man, to say something appropriately great. It is the ritual of human sacrifice, and the fillet adorns my brow. Although I have come to this altar without unseemly struggle, it is not with peace of mind. All the great things were said about Shakespeare a great many years ago, and by poets not professors. I shall quote them in conclusion. My problem has been to find something to say before I reach the conclusion, and I am happy to announce that I have found a solution.

As you all know, not a single letter written by Shakespeare has been at the disposal of his biographers. It occurred to me that it might be acceptable to you if I found a modest sheaf of such letters and read them to you, thus letting Shakespeare speak for himself on what kind of man he was. Having eight days free at mid-year, when I would not be writing essays for memorial volumes, I flew to England (on one of the academic economy charter flights) and conducted an intensive search. Eight days may not seem much time, but I had the inspired idea of looking only in such places as had not been searched before, thus narrowing the field considerably. With the incentive provided by the present impending occasion, my efforts were strenuous and crowned by a fair degree of success. Although I found only three letters, I was able to obtain possession and thus circumvent any difficulties about permission to make them public. The letters are undated, but by establishing a background chronology (as only a literary historian like myself could do) I can provide you with the approximate times of composition. This first letter— to his wife—was obviously written in 1593–94 between the publication of *Venus and Adonis* and the publication of *The Rape of Lucrece*. It is superscribed—

To be delivered to Mistress Agnes, dwelling with Master John Shakespeare, at the sign of the Compass in Henley Street.

Now I realize that you, as the first audience ever to hear the reading of an original Shakespeare letter, may be waiting with a certain sense of impatience and anxiety, and I do not wish to encumber you with a series of textual notes, but I must point out that the names "Agnes" and "Anne" (or, variantly, "Annes") were interchangeable, so that the occurrence here of "Agnes" casts no shadow whatever upon the authenticity of this document. It proceeds—in somewhat difficult, but by no means untutored, English secretary hand:

My Loving Partner, I send thee all commendations, with the pledge of a loving heart, trusting in God that all thine and mine are in health; and by this bearer, who is a trusty tenant of Lord Dudley's at Claverdon, a budget of fairings from London. Receive it with these letters, as also the pamphlet and the purse. The angels lay by until my coming in Lent, when we will speak further of thy removal. The purse with the King Edward groats for my boy, when my girls are going fine in the new caps, and tell him to wear it nobly for 'tis a noble purse. My fine-printed poem to be seen, but not handed about, and then laid up in the coffer where is the silver christening-cup. My news is all good news. The sickness hath continued to abate, and the privy council hath recalled our restraint, so that we are playing again in Shore-ditch with good auditories and approval. The four angels are the golden fruit fetched home from my voyage to Southampton his lordship's favor, whither I was guided by Dick Fields, who hath been a kind and careful friend to his countryman and old school-fellow all during the inhibition. With the two pounds allowed me by Dick for the copy, his Lordship's four angels bring my guerdon for the poem to four pounds—or eighty shillings—or nearly a thousand pence. Would 't were a thousand pounds! Dick now hath my Lucrece in hand, which will be vended by Master Har-rison. The poem is graver, the dedication longer, and perchance the purse will be heavier. If his Lordship is grateful to the sum of six or eight angels, we will have our earnest of a house this year in despite of the pestilence. Master Burbage assures us that we will have our license, and I my market for my wares, so that I must needs be an arch dedicating poet no longer. In Lent, my sweeting, I will read thee Lucrece, and a good Lenten tale it is, and I trust to our dear Redeemer thou wilt not mistake me for Tarquin, with a taste for ravishing chaste wives. I am not the man. When I read thee the papers of the tale which now I send, and awaited thy plaudite, I well remember that thy only word was to ask me if I had made Adonis to scorn Venus because she was an older woman. I prithee, dear wife, be not a simple woman, or like those who think Ned Alleyn a monstrous villain because he played bad Barabbas. We players and poets are strange fellows who are the better the better we feign. Venus was no woman but a naughty goddess, and Adon was turned into a wind-flower, as, God knoweth, I am not like to be though my petals are falling fast. And I prithee, dear wife, cease vexing thyself about the small advantage of years thou hast of me, and cease asking me if thou art fading. So must we all, but love's not time's fool though rosy lips and cheeks within his bending sickle's compass come. I will conster this for thee when we meet and kiss, until when know, as I know, that thou wilt always have—Thy Will.

Not the least interesting feature of this letter is the way it provides a hint of the origin of the legend that Southampton gave Shakespeare the preposterously large sum of a thousand pounds. You will have noticed the whimsical allusion to a thousand pence. Speaking of money, let me say that I have the impression that the three letters I have found have a substantial monetary value. However, since they have already amply rewarded me by rescuing me from a tight place, I have decided to give them away. This one, to Anne, strikes me as very English in its sturdy domesticity and I think it should go back to England—somewhere near the heartland. I am at present undecided between the Birthplace Trust and the Bodleian Library, but it will probably be the latter—where the students once pored over the love scenes in the newly acquired First Folio, and where perchance now some Oxford undergraduate (or even some Fellow of a college) may widen his horizons by contemplating this letter.

The next letter, though considerably shorter, has also its interesting features. Addressed to Shakespeare's one-time neighbor and the probable godfather of his son, it can be dated by internal evidence 1600–1601:

To Hamnet Sadler, at High and Sheep Street next the Corn Market, deliver these.
Good friend and countryman, your letters have come to me by the hand of Gilbert, and I know not why you reproach me. The ten pounds I sent thee were hard come by, and lent thee at nothing on the hundred, as was all else which you have had of me sith thy fire. You tell me of the thirty pounds with which I friended Master Quiney when he was here on the business of the charter, and the thirty pounds had of me by Master Sturley, but these moneys were taken on security, and Master Quiney hath repaid me, as hath Master Sturley in part. Would to God my countrymen would not use me as their factor, for it is costly, and I have great expenses, and my Susan and Judith to dower. My loving friend, I do truly sorrow for thy afflictions, and I know of thy many children with the fine boy named for me, but our town is filled with the needy, most of them my kinsmen. Know then that I will add

still ten pounds more to that which thou hast already had, but that it must be the last until something is repaid, and to signify that you will keep faith with me in this, subscribe your name to this paper and take it to Newplace, where you will be delivered the sum from my coffers there. The Lord be with you and yours and with us all, amen. I am about a new play upon thy namesake, Hamlet the Dane, and was driving my pen with great joy and alacrity when Gilbert brought thy letters, which so dash my spirits that I must give Hamlet o'er till I feel somewhat less melancholy. The whilst I am heavy I will work upon my Merry Wives of Windsor which was promised the people a twelve-month ago. May thine own Wife be merry and thy fortunes mend. In all kindness—thy Will Shakespeare.

Although the situation which occasioned the above letter was, understandably, depressing, I should hesitate to conclude that it initiated in the dramatist's career a "tragic period"—especially if Sadler kept the bargain to refrain from further attack. (The letter bears the requested endorsement.) All three letters, although sent to different addresses in Stratford, contain clues suggesting that they must one time have been among the muniments of New Place and hence why I found them together. Since the one just read shows Shakespeare playing the role of banker, however ungladly, and employs the word "dower," I have decided that an appropriate permanent home for it would be right here in the Pierpont Morgan Library.

The final letter is especially interesting, since it was obviously written in 1611–12, on the eve of Shakespeare's retirement. The recipient was the most literary of his Stratford circle, the former Middle Templer Thomas Greene, his kinsman and, for a while, a lodger at New Place:

To the hand of Thomas Greene, Esquire, dwelling at St. Mary's house near the Church.

All happiness to my dear cousin and to my cousin's dear Lettice. I will, as I foretold thee, be in Stratford by Shrovetide, and a homekeeper ever after. My grapevines and roses, and my new-planted mulberry, await their careful Adam. And yet methinks, friend Tom, that if I spend all my hours a-pruning them, perchance I shall prune too close, besides the which, when the rain rains and the wind blows cold December, I must do my delving indoors, and therefore I am increasing my store of books. This day I bought the new Bible in folio, and the History of the World by Sir Walter, also in folio, and these with other, and with my Chronicles, bring my books in folio to the number of twelve, and there may be still one more as I shall presently tell thee. And so, good cousin, please to do me the service of stopping at Newplace, and bidding Hickox my joiner, who is at work there, that when he comes to erect in the nook of my study the press-cupboard glazed with the six shelves, that the shelves must not be at the marks I did formerly set him, but must be with the two lower-most shelves two spans in height instead of the lowermost shelf alone, and with the other shelves new spaced as shown in the drawing on this margent. I trouble thee with this because my son Hall may be from home, and Hickox is slow of wit, and my women not like to make him understand this matter even if they understand it themselves. And for thy reward I will tell thee of a meeting of the poets at the Mermaid, whither we two sometimes went for a sherris in thy days at the Temple. I had been at Paul's searching out copies of my plays in print to bring with me as remembrancers, since all my playbooks must abide here with the company, and I had in my hand four or five such, which caused great merriment when I came upon some at the tavern. Ben Jonson was there, and he asked wittily if the stationers would be making of my plays another Bible in folio, whereupon Tom Dekker, who is always girding at him, asked how many lines he would first have me blot, so rubbing an old sore, and Ben grew choleric and made biting jests upon Master Dekker and upon me and my plays, and then grew surly silent. One Tom Heywood, whom you know not since he writ not for our company though a good playmaker (if no Orpheus) and a good man, was there with the rest, and now said gentle things to restore fellowship, among them that he had in hand the writing of a book of the lives of all the poets, and not ancient poets alone, for in it would be Kit Marlowe, and Ben Jonson, and Will Shakespeare too. This I, taking in jest, though honest Heywood meant it not so, said I would give over my page in his book because my plays had returned to me good things enough. They had given me joy in the making, had won me bread, and had pleased the people. Whereupon our Ben raised his eyes from his tankard where they were bent in the dumps, and said that which amazed the company and touched my heart. Master Will, said he, thy plays will one day be printed indeed in folio—and prized—and one day a whole book will be written about thy plays alone. And so, my dear Tom, tell Lettice, without envy, of the fame in store for thy cousin Will, and tell Hickox to make the press-cupboard wide so that my folio may stand next the new Bible (God pardon the jest) with room enough for that whole book which will one day be written about my art. Farewell until I come to thee with the spring. Thy loving kinsman—Will.

I think the best place for this letter, dealing as it does with the problem of shelving a possible "folio" as well as a "whole book" about Shakespeare's art, would be the Folger Library.

Now it may be that the epistolary style of these letters may suggest some lesser man, such as Edward Alleyn, but we must remember that even the greatest of literary geniuses will have relaxed moments when he does not compose at the top of his bent. If picayune skeptics express doubts about the authenticity of these letters, I shall merely point out that their data dovetail perfectly with all the biographical evidence previously at our disposal, and that their tone is in accord with what is known of the man through his works—that he was a devoted *family man* (as witness every play as well as the biographical documents), that he was a *tolerant and generous* man (even though he husbanded his hard-won gains), and that he was a *modest* man (one of whose last words to us was the request that we forgive him his artistic trespasses).

What else was Shakespeare? Here I shall turn to documents of more firmly established provenance than those I have been reading, and quote half a dozen of what I consider the finest things ever said about him—all of them brief and all of them very familiar. The first two are by that strangely tortured man of integrity Ben Jonson:

. . . I loved the man, and do honor his memory (on this side idolatry) as much as any. He was indeed honest, and of an open and free nature: he had an excellent fancy, brave notions, and gentle expressions. . . .

These words were written privately, almost in self-communion, and so intended to impress no one—and yet who could ask for a lovelier epitaph. The words "honest" and "gentle" have lost their edge since Jonson's day, have been sentimentalized. Jonson himself, as he told Drummond, wished of all things to be called "honest," and he used the word when distinguishing between true literary craftsmen and hacks. An earlier spokesman called Shakespeare the actor "excellent in the quality he professes"—a good workman. And so thought Jonson. Shakespeare was a good workman in letters, in part because he was a good man. He was "honest." He delivered more than he was paid for. Then there is Jonson's public tribute "To the Memory of my beloved, The Author. Mr. William Shakespeare: And what he has left us"—"Soule of the Age,/The applause! delight! the wonder of our Stage!"

> He was not of an age, but for all time,
> And all the Muses still were in their prime,
> When, like Apollo, he came forth to warm
> Our ears or like a Mercury to charm.

Jonson was not the easiest of men to warm or to charm, but Shakespeare succeeded with him as with the penny-playgoers, and as he has been warming and charming the whole world since.

Next, John Dryden's almost casual dictum: "To begin then

with Shakespeare; he was the man who of all Modern, and perhaps Ancient Poets, had the largest and most comprehensive soul." For a person like Dryden to speak thus of a poet of the rude age last past, and to place him (even with the qualifying "perhaps") above his beloved Homer, Vergil, and Horace, was a tribute as magnanimous as Ben's—and as inevitable. Next there is the second Johnson, the one who spelled his name correctly:

Nothing can please many and please long but just representations of general nature. . . . The pleasures of sudden wonder are soon exhausted, and the mind can only repose on the stability of truth. Shakespeare is above all writers, at least above all modern writers, the poet of nature; the poet that holds up to his readers a faithful mirror of manners and of life.

There is still the cautious refusal to lurch the laurel outright from the Ancients, but the good doctor went as far in this direction as a man of his background could go.

It is strange. The greatest of the early tributes to our leading romantic poet came from the greatest of our classicists, and Pope's voice chimes with theirs. Still it is the word of another romantic which touches the profoundest truth:

A man's life of any worth is a continual allegory—and very few eyes can see the mystery of his life—a life like the scriptures figurative. . . . Shakespeare lived a life of allegory and his works are the comments on it.

Keats perceived that the passage through life which began four centuries ago was the journey of an Everyman figure— the only one we have had who was big enough for the role. Finally I shall quote lines which make no mention of Shakespeare, but which might well have been addressed directly to the man who personifies their theme. The good Heywood never got around to completing his "Lives of All the Poets," but Samuel Daniel published his *Musophilus* on the eve of

the appearance of the great tragedies. Chaucer, Sidney, and
Spenser appear in Daniel's roll of honor, but none of the
poets whose work was not yet wholly done. Still these lines
belong to Shakespeare:

> O blessed letters, that combine in one
> All ages past, and make one live with all,
> By you we do confer with who are gone
> And the dead-living unto counsel call:
> By you th' unborn shall have communion
> Of what we feel, and what doth us befall.

NOTES

I A LIFE OF ALLEGORY

1. Letter to William Sandys, June 13, 1847, *Letters of Charles Dickens*, ed. G. Hogarth and M. Dickens (London and New York, 1893), p. 173.

2. Anthony Scoloker, Epistle to *Daiphantus* (1604); cf. E. K. Chambers, *William Shakespeare*, 2 vols. (Oxford, 1930), II, 214.

3. *Timber: or Discoveries* (1641), ed. C. H. Herford and Percy and Evelyn Simpson, *Ben Jonson*, vol. VIII (Oxford, 1947), p. 583.

4. John Dryden, *Of Dramatick Poesie*, 1668, p. 50.

5. "Letter from Mr. G. Bernard Shaw," in Leo Tolstoy, *Tolstoy on Shakespeare* (New York, 1906).

6. Benjamin Bailey to R. M. Milnes, May 7, 1849, *The Keats Circle*, ed. Hyder Edward Rollins, 2 vols. (Cambridge, Mass., 1948), II, 271–272.

7. Sir Sidney Lee, *A Life of William Shakespeare*, 1898 (New York, 1916), pp. 500–501.

8. J. Dover Wilson, *The Essential Shakespeare* (Cambridge, 1932), p. 6.

9. Clara Longworth de Chambrun, *Shakespeare, Actor-Poet* (New York and London, 1927), p. 17.

10. John Bunyan, *The Pilgrim's Progress* (1678), ed. J. B. Wharey, 2nd ed., rev. by R. Sharrock (Oxford, 1960), p. 154.

11. J. Dover Wilson, *The Meaning of* The Tempest, Robert Spence Watson Memorial Lecture (Newcastle upon Tyne, 1936), p. 21.

12. Blaise Pascal, *The Pensées*, trans. J. M. Cohen (Penguin Classics, 1961), p. 39.

13. To George and Georgiana Keats, Feb. 19, 1819, *Letters of John Keats*, ed. Hyder Edward Rollins, 2 vols. (Cambridge, Mass., 1958), II, 67.

2 THE MYTH OF PERFECTION

1. *The Works of Shakespeare*, 7 vols. (London, 1733), I, 319, 321.

2. The quoted comments illustrate my point whoever made them, but I hope I am citing the right persons. They are attributed to

Whalley and Malone in *The Plays of William Shakespeare,* 15 vols. (London, 1793), IV, 205, and in subsequent "variorum" editions by Isaac Reed, James Boswell, etc., but I do not find the comment by Whalley in his *Enquiry* (London, 1748), while Malone makes a different and more judicious comment in *The Plays and Poems of William Shakespeare,* 10 vols. (London, 1790), II, 19.

3. *The Works of Shakespeare,* ed. W. G. Clark, J. Glover, and W. A. Wright, 9 vols. (Cambridge & London, 1863–66), I, xii.

4. See note 2, above.

5. *Measure for Measure* (Cambridge 1922), p. 122.

6. *Measure for Measure,* Arden edition (London, 1905, revised 1925), p. 16.

7. E. K. Chambers, *William Shakespeare* (Oxford, 1930), I, 231.

8. *2 Henry IV,* ed. M. A. Shaaber (Philadelphia, 1940), p. 132.

9. E. K. Chambers; *Shakespeare,* I, 231.

10. Fleay's comment is quoted from *Robinson's Epitomy of Literature,* 1 April 1879, by H. H. Furness in the New Variorum edition of *A Midsummer Night's Dream* (Philadelphia, 1895), p. 298.

11. The familiar wording is from the *Literary Remains* edited by H. N. Coleridge in 1836. Samuel Coleridge seems actually to have said, "The task [of criticizing Shakespeare] will be genial in proportion as the criticism is reverential." See *Coleridge's Shakespearean Criticism,* ed. T. M. Raysor, 2 vols. (Cambridge, Mass., 1930), I, 126.

3 THESE OUR ACTORS

1. "Shakespeare Foundation Schools," *The Speeches of Charles Dickens,* ed. K. J. Fielding (Oxford, 1960), pp. 335–36.

2. Anthony Aston, *A Brief Supplement to Colley Cibber, Esq.,* ed. R. W. Lowe, in *An Apology for the Life of Mr. Colley Cibber, Comedian* (London, 1889), II, 307. The author (who genuinely admired Betterton) adds that he was "clumsily made, having a great head, a short thick neck, stoop'd in the shoulders, and had fat short arms . . . He had little eyes and a broad face, a little pock-fretten, a corpulent body, and thick legs, with large feet."

3. *King Richard the Second,* V, ii, 23–26:

> As in a theatre the eyes of men,
> After a well-graced actor leaves the stage,
> Are idly bent on him that enters next,
> Thinking his prattle to be tedious . . .

4. Harley Granville-Barker, *Prefaces to Shakespeare, Third Series: Hamlet* (London, 1937), p. 5.

5. See Sir Walter Scott's remarks on Kemble's Macbeth and Hotspur, *Miscellaneous Prose Works* (Edinburgh and London, 1835), XX, 191–93.

6. *Recollections of the Life of John O'Keeffe*, 2 vols. (London, 1826), I, 81.

7. Charles Dickens, "Mr. Fechter's Acting," *Atlantic Monthly*, August 1889, *The Nonesuch Dickens Collected Papers*, 2 vols. (Bloomsbury, 1937), I, 124–25.

8. Leigh Hunt, *Dramatic Essays*, ed. W. Archer & R. W. Lowe (London, 1894), p. 206.

9. *An Apology for the Life of Mr. Colley Cibber, Comedian* (1740), ed. R. W. Lowe, I, 159.

10. Charles Dickens, "The Restoration of Shakespeare's 'Lear' to the Stage," *The Examiner*, Feb. 8, 1838, *The Nonesuch Dickens Collected Papers*, I, 124–25.

11. Anonymous, *A Letter to Miss Nossiter, occasioned by her first appearance on the stage* (London, 1753), p. 13.

12. E. K. Chambers, *The Elizabethan Stage*, 4 vols. (Oxford, 1923), II, 309.

13. Walt Whitman, "The Old Bowery," in *November Boughs* (1888), *Complete Prose Works* (New York, 1914), p. 430.

4 WEIGHING DELIGHT AND DOLE

1. W. Bridges-Adams, *The Irresistible Theatre* (New York, 1957).

2. Henry Howes, "How to Use Shakespeare," *Saturday Review*, July 13, 1957, pp. 10–13.

3. Edward Sharpham, *The Fleir* (1607), cited in *The Shakespere Allusion-Book*, ed. John Munro, 2 vols. (London, 1909), I, 174.

4. *The Observer*, September 16, 1962.

5. *King Lear*, III, vii, 99–107.

5 THE FIERCE DISPUTE

1. I have discussed these more fully, though still inadequately, in *Shakespeare: The Tragedies*, an anthology of criticism in the series *Twentieth Century Views*, ed. Maynard Mack (Englewood Cliffs, N. J., 1964), pp. 1–9.

2. See above, p. 50.

3. "An English Interior in the Seventeenth Century," *British Quarterly Review*, LV, 64 (January 1872).

4. Nahum Tate, Dedication to Thomas Boteler, *The History of King Lear, Acted at the Queen's Theatre*, revised, with alterations, by N. Tate (London, 1681).

5. Charles B. Hogan, *Shakespeare in the Theatre, 1701–1800*, 2 vols. (Oxford, 1952–1957).

6. Nicholas Rowe, *The Works of Mr. William Shakespear*, revised edition, 9 vols. (London, 1714), IX, pp. xxiii, 359.

7. Thomas Cooke, *Considerations on the Stage and on the Advantages which Arise to a Nation from the Encouragement of the Arts* (London, 1731), p. 55.

8. Johnson and Steevens' edition of the *Works*, ed. Isaac Reed, the "First Variorum," 21 vols. (London, 1803), XVII, 612. Steevens says, "The altered play has the upper gallery on its side; the original drama was patronized by Addison." But Tate's plaudits came not only from the "upper gallery."

9. John Upton, *Critical Observations on Shakespeare* (London, 1746).

10. Thomas Edwards, *Canons of Criticism* (1748), 6th ed. (London, 1758), pp. 230–36; Elizabeth Montagu, *An Essay on the Writings and Genius of Shakespear* (London, 1769), *passim; The Tragedies of Sophocles*, trans. Thomas Francklin (London, 1758), *passim*.

11. Thomas Davies, *Dramatic Miscellanies*, 3 vols. (London, 1784), II, 267, 318.

12. Joseph Warton, *The Adventurer*, No. 122 (Jan. 5, 1754).

13. Edward Taylor, *Cursory Remarks on Tragedy, on Shakespear, and on certain French and Italian Poets, principally Tragedians* (London, 1774), p. 46.

14. *Works of Shakespeare*, ed. Reed, XVII, 612.

15. *The Spectator*, Nos. 39 and 40 (April 14 and 16, 1711).

16. David Hume, "Of Tragedy," *Four Dissertations* (London, 1757).

17. See the précis of Schiller's views in René Wellek, *A History of Modern Criticism: 1750–1950*, 2 vols. (New Haven, 1955), I, 247–250.

18. Montagu, *Essay on the Writings of Shakespear*, p. 40.

19. A. W. Schlegel, *A Course of Lectures on Dramatic Art and Literature* (1808), trans. John Black, 1815 (Philadelphia, 1833), p. 337.

20. Charles Lamb, *Poems, Plays and Miscellaneous Essays*, ed. A. Ainger (London, 1895), p. 234.

21. *Ibid.*, pp. 233–234.
22. *Blackwood's Edinburgh Magazine*, V, 228 (May 1819).
23. William Hazlitt, *Characters of Shakespear's Plays* (New York, 1845), p. 103.
24. *Letters of John Keats*, ed. H. E. Rollins, 2 vols. (Cambridge, Mass., 1958), I, 192.
25. *Ibid.*, I, 210.
26. *Ibid.*, I, 232.
27. *Ibid.*, II, 101–102.
28. See above, p. 48.
29. *Coleridge's Writings on Shakespeare*, ed. T. Hawkes (New York, 1959), 178–188.
30. H. N. Hudson, *Lectures on Shakespeare*, 2 vols. (New York, 1848).
31. Edward Dowden, *Shakspere: A Critical Study of His Mind and Art*, 1875 (London, 1948), pp. 263, 272.
32. A. C. Bradley, *Shakespearean Tragedy*, 1904 (London, 1950), p. 285.
33. G. Wilson Knight, *The Wheel of Fire*, 1930 (London, 1949).
34. R. W. Chambers, *King Lear: The First W. P. Ker Memorial Lecture* (Glasgow, 1940), pp. 35–38.
35. H. B. Charlton, *Shakespearian Tragedy* (Cambridge, 1948), p. 227.
36. Arthur Sewell, *Character and Society in Shakespeare* (Oxford, 1951), p. 84.
37. *Ibid.*, pp. 91, 108.
38. Edward Dowden, *Shakespere*, p. 265.
39. A. C. Bradley, *Shakespearean Tragedy*, p. 279.
40. H. B. Charlton, *Shakespearian Tragedy*, p. 213.
41. *Coleridge's Writings on Shakespeare*, p. 178.
42. Sigmund Freud, *Collected Papers*, IV (New York, 1924), 236.
43. *King Lear*, ed. H. N. Hudson (Boston, 1879).
44. Richard B. Sewell, *The Vision of Tragedy* (New Haven, 1959), p. 78.
45. Arthur Sewell, *Character and Society in Shakespeare*, p. 121.
46. J. C. Maxwell, "The Technique of Invocation in 'King Lear'," *Modern Language Review*, XLV, 142 (April 1950).

6 SHAKESPEARE AS CULTURE HERO

1. William F. and Elizebeth S. Friedman, *The Shakespearean*

Ciphers Examined (Cambridge, 1957); Frank W. Wadsworth, *The Poacher from Stratford* (Berkeley, 1958); R. C. Churchill, *Shakespeare and His Betters* (London, 1958); H. N. Gibson, *The Shakespeare Claimants* (London, 1962); Milward W. Martin, *Was Shakespeare Shakespeare?* (New York, 1965).

2. Lord Raglan, *The Hero: A Study in Tradition, Myth, and Drama* (London, 1949). Although indebted to this book for its data on the parallel careers of mythological heroes, I cannot endorse, or indeed quite understand, its thesis on the origins of drama in ritual.

3. Otto Rank, *The Myth of the Birth of the Hero and Other Writings,* ed. Philip Freund (New York, 1959).

4. Dryden by letters patent, Jonson and Davenant by the implication of royal patronage and pensions.

5. First recorded by Richard Davies after 1688; cf. E. K. Chambers, *William Shakespeare* (Oxford, 1930), II, 255-257.

6. *The Tragedies of Sophocles,* trans. and ed. Thomas Francklin (London, 1788), p. 61.

7. Listed as earlier doubters, but with insufficient reason, are James Townley and Herbert Lawrence. Townley's *High Life Below Stairs* (1759) satirizes the illiterate pretense of servants who mistake the name of an author for a title:

[MAID]: Shikspur. Did you never read *Shikspur?*
KITTY: *Shikspur? Shikspur?*—Who wrote it?

(The item is described correctly by Wadsworth, p. 11; incorrectly by Churchill, p. 30, who attributes to the farce of 1759 matter which does not appear in it, but which may have been added later.) Lawrence's *The Life and Adventures of Common Sense* (1769) belongs to an eighteenth-century genre of satirical social commentary presented through allegorical travels (e.g., of a penny) and has no bearing on the authorship question.

8. By A. B. Cornwall (Birmingham, Eng., 1936).

9. The first formal denial of Shakespeare's authorship in print appeared in Joseph C. Hart's *The Romance of Yachting* (New York, 1848), pp. 208-242. Then came Delia Bacon's essay in *Putnam's Monthly Magazine,* VII (1856), 1-19, followed by her *The Philosophy of the Plays of Shakespeare Unfolded* (London, 1857). Contemporary with these were Henry Smith's published letter to Lord Ellesmere proposing Bacon as author in 1856, followed in the same year by his small book *Was Bacon the Author of Shakespeare's Plays?* "scooping" Delia Bacon's. Although these were the earliest overt anti-

Stratfordian treatises, an undercurrent of dissatisfaction with the humble Shakespeare may have existed for some time; a character in Disraeli's *Venetia* (1837) expresses a doubt that he ever wrote "a single whole play."

10. The priority of Wilmot was noted by Allardyce Nicoll, "The First Baconian," *Times Literary Supplement,* Feb. 25, 1932. The frauds of his niece, Olivia Wilmot Serres, are described in the *Dictionary of National Biography* and in William J. Thoms, *Hannah Lightfoot* (London, 1867). Not previously discussed in connection with her inventions, so far as I know, is the romance by "Olivia W. S———," *Memoirs of a Princess, or First Love* (London, 1812), a copy of which in the Widener Library contains her autograph and the bookplate of Lord Eglintin, one of her noble backers. The story is a thinly disguised account of a youthful love affair of Caroline of Brunswick (here called "Dantzwick") before her marriage to George IV. The implication is that this prior commitment caused the failure of her marriage to "the most accomplished and powerful sovereign of the world" (II, 156). "How greatly is the Prince of B——— to be pitied . . . united to one *whose heart is another's!*" (II, 133). Olivia was herself infatuated with the Prince Regent. His morganatic marriage with Maria Fitzherbert in 1785 seems to have provided her with the material for her story that James Wilmot had married the Regent's father, George III, to the "fair quaker" Hannah Lightfoot, and then remarried him to his queen. Olivia's *Memoirs of a Princess,* like her *St. Julian* (1805), is highly derivative. Despite her claim to royal birth, backed by forged documents, she was not truly inventive.

11. See Vivian C. Hopkins, *Prodigal Puritan: A Life of Delia Bacon* (Cambridge, Mass., 1959). The book is sympathetic, but the facts speak for themselves.

12. Hopkins, p. 252.

13. Mark Twain, *Is Shakespeare Dead? From My Autobiography* (New York, 1909).

14. Van Wyck Brooks, *The Ordeal of Mark Twain* (New York, 1955), pp. 52, 188.

15. *Mark Twain–Howells Letters,* ed. Henry Nash Smith and William M. Gibson (Cambridge, Mass., 1960), II, 533–534.

16. He publicly referred to his conversion in accepting the Goethe Prize at Weimar in 1930; cf. *Gesammelte Schriften von Sigm. Freud,* XII (Vienna, 1934), 410.

17. *Sigmund Freud, An Autobiographical Study,* trans. James

Strachey in *Complete Psychological Works,* XX (1935), 63–64; *An Outline of Psychoanalysis,* trans. James Strachey (New York, 1944), p. 96.

18. Sigmund Freud, *Collected Papers,* ed. James Strachey, V (London, 1950), 76.

19. Ernest Jones, *The Life and Work of Sigmund Freud* (New York, 1953–1957), III, 428–430.

7 SHAKESPEARE'S IDEAL MAN

1. *Life and Writings of Joseph Mazzini,* 6 vols. (London, 1890–91), vol. II, p. viii.
2. *Ibid.,* II, 89.
3. *Ibid.,* II, 133-34.
4. George Santayana, *Interpretations of Poetry and Religion,* in *Works,* vol. II (New York, 1936), p. iii.
5. Mazzini, *Life and Writings,* II, 135.
6. *Ibid.,* II, 147.
7. T. S. Eliot, "Shakespeare and the Stoicism of Seneca" (1927), in *Selected Essays* (London, 1951), pp. 126–40.
8. G. B. Shaw, "Better than Shakespear?" *Three Plays for Puritans* (New York, 1906), p. xxx.
9. Edward Dowden, *Shakespere: A Critical Study of His Mind and Art,* 1875 (London, 1948), p. 40.
10. *Julius Caesar,* V, v, 68–75. (Quotations and citations from Shakespeare are from *The Pelican Shakespeare,* Penguin Books.)
11. *Hamlet,* V, ii, 384–89.
12. *All's Well,* I, i, 90.
13. *Ibid.,* I, ii, 31–48.
14. *Hamlet,* III, ii, 60–71.
15. *Ibid.,* III, i, 151–53.
16. *Romeo and Juliet,* III, v, 181–84.
17. *Twelfth Night,* I, v, 244–48.
18. *Troilus and Cressida,* I, ii, 239–42.
19. *Two Gentlemen,* III, ii, 32.
20. *Twelfth Night,* III, iv, 334–37.
21. *Merchant of Venice,* I, ii, 104.
22. *Measure for Measure,* III, ii, 136–37.
23. *Two Gentlemen,* I, ii, 10; I, iii, 1–34; V, ii, 1–30; *Henry V,* II, ii, 127–40; *As You Like It,* I, i, 153–56; *Much Ado,* II, i, 336–38;

III, i, 96; *Twelfth Night*, I, v, 86–91; *Julius Caesar*, III, i, 126–27; *Hamlet*, I, iii, 55–81; I, v, 140–42; *Troilus and Cressida*, IV, v, 96–107; *Macbeth*, III, i, 51–54; IV, iii, 9–96; *Antony and Cleopatra*, V, ii, 83–92; *Winter's Tale*, I, ii, 389–92; *Cymbeline*, I, i, 28–55; etc.

24. *Hamlet*, V, ii, 215–26.
25. *Shakespeare's Works*, ed. Isaac Reed (London, 1803), XVIII, 367n.
26. *Hamlet*, ed. G. L. Kittredge (Boston, 1939), p. 98.
27. *Hamlet*, III, ii, 321–22.
28. *Hamlet*, ed. H. H. Furness (New Variorum Edition, 1877), I, 266–67.
29. *2 Henry VI*, II, i, 49.
30. *1 Henry IV*, II, iv, 560.
31. *Henry V*, IV, vii, 145–50.
32. *Merchant of Venice*, II, i, 20–22.
33. *Winter's Tale*, III, ii, 201–02.
34. *Antony and Cleopatra*, II, iii, 6–7, 38–39.
35. *Winter's Tale*, V, i, 133–46.
36. *All's Well*, I, iii, 184–242.
37. *Twelfth Night*, I, v, 320.
38. *Merchant of Venice*, III, iv, 26–34.
39. *Romeo and Juliet*, III, v; IV, ii, 17–22; IV, iii, 1–12.
40. *Ibid.*, IV, v, 65–70.
41. *Much Ado*, IV, i, 200–06; V, iv, 69.
42. *Measure for Measure*, V, i, 150–62.
43. *Hamlet*, III, i, 131.
44. *Othello*, III, iv, 23–24.
45. *Coriolanus*, III, ii, 52–64.
46. *Othello*, V, ii, 124.
47. *Julius Caesar*, II, i, 127–29.
48. *Cymbeline*, IV, ii, 377–79.
49. *Measure for Measure*, II, ii, 99–101; see also II, i, 1–31.
50. *Hamlet*, II, ii, 515–17.
51. In *All's Well that Ends Well*.
52. *King Lear*, III, iv, 32–36.
53. Mazzini, *Life and Writings*, II, 209.
54. Thomas Otway, "The Poet's Complaint to his Muse."
55. John Dryden, "Alexander's Feast."

INDEX

INDEX

INDEX

INDEX

INDEX